How to be a Brilliant FE Teacher

How to be a Brilliant FE Teacher is a straightforward, friendly guide to being an effective and innovative teacher in post-compulsory education. Focusing on practical advice drawn from the author's extensive and successful personal experience of both teaching and training teachers, it offers sound guidance, underpinned by the latest research, theory and policy in the field.

Structured around the questions that all new teachers and lecturers ask in their first teaching post, it is an introduction to both essential teaching skills and what to expect from working in this exciting, fast-paced sector. Key chapters cover:

- The learners – who they are, diversity and motivation
- What will actually happen – organising teaching, technology and resources
- How to keep your students' interest – understanding and responding to learning styles
- How you'll know your students are learning – assessment and feedback
- Ensuring teaching is effective – student evaluation, reflecting on and improving practice.

Packed throughout with information about where to find the best materials and resources to support your teaching, this book also offers sensible advice on balancing home and life, working effectively with your colleagues and progressing in your career.

How to be a Brilliant FE Teacher will be a source of support and inspiration for all those embarking on their initial training and first post in the sector, as well as qualified professionals looking for reassuring, fresh ideas.

Vicky Duckworth is Senior Lecturer and MA Co-ordinator in Post Compulsory Education and Training and Schools' University Lead at Edge Hill University, UK.

E-resources are available at www.routledge.com/books/details/9780415519021/

How to be a Brilliant FE Teacher

A practical guide to being effective and innovative

Vicky Duckworth

Routledge
Taylor & Francis Group

LONDON AND NEW YORK

First published 2014
by Routledge
2 Park Square, Milton Park, Abingdon, Oxon OX14 4RN

Simultaneously published in the USA and Canada
by Routledge
711 Third Avenue, New York, NY 10017

Routledge is an imprint of the Taylor & Francis Group, an informa
business

British Library Cataloguing in Publication Data
A catalogue record for this book is available from the British
Library

Library of Congress Cataloging in Publication Data
Duckworth, Vicky.
   How to be a brilliant FE teacher : a practical guide to being
effective and innovative / authored by Vicky Duckworth.
      pages cm
   Includes index.
   1. Continuing education—Great Britain.   2. Teaching—Great
Britain.   I. Title.
   LC5256.G7D83 2013
   374.941—dc23

                                              2013006789

ISBN: 978-0-415-51901-4 (hbk)
ISBN: 978-0-415-51902-1 (pbk)
ISBN: 978-0-203-12283-9 (ebk)

Typeset in Sabon
by RefineCatch Limited, Bungay, Suffolk

MIX
Paper from
responsible sources
FSC
www.fsc.org   FSC® C013056

Printed and bound in Great Britain by
TJ International Ltd, Padstow, Cornwall

With love to mam and dad, Anne Duckworth
(née Macauley) and Harry Duckworth

Contents

Acknowledgements

The academy is not paradise. But learning is a place where paradise can be created. The classroom with all its limitations remains a location of possibility. In that field of possibility we have the opportunity to labour for freedom, to demand of ourselves and our comrades, an openness of mind and heart that allows us to face reality even as we collectively imagine ways to move beyond boundaries, to transgress. This is education as the practice of freedom.

bell hooks 1994: 207

I would like to thank my students who have been an inspiration in many ways, and the brilliant teachers who are listed in the chapters and have generously contributed case studies to this book. Thanks to family and friends: Craig Ludlow, Anna and Niamh Ludlow, Mary Hamilton, Jonathan Tummons, Steve Ingle, Mike Austin, Sue Watmore, Janet Lord, Carmel Gibbons, Paula Bithells, Sandra Robinson, Marie and Chris Ludlow, Michelle Stephens, Sharon Fitzpatrick, Liz Thomas and Maxine Williamson for sharing the tapestry of life.

Thanks to all my colleagues whose commitment to excellence is tireless: Robert Smedley (Dean Of Education), Margaret Postance and the PCET team: Jane, John, Lindsey, Mike, the Schools' University Steering group: Peter, Chris, Polly, Kathy, Dawne, Roger and all the staff in the Faculty of Education at Edge Hill University.

Case study contributor, Mike Bailey, would like to thank his inspirational former teacher Gwen Middlehurst who taught at Priestley College in Warrington for many years and inspired him to be a brilliant teacher.

Brilliant teaching is based on mutual respect and strong professional relationships between the teacher and the learners. The teacher needs to demonstrate outstanding levels of planning, preparation and organisation which demonstrate their mastery as educational leaders, and which provide opportunities for learners to fully engage with their learning as active participants. The resulting learning needs to be interesting, varied and relevant to all, resulting in the highest possible outcome, both personally and academically.

Margaret Postance, Head of Post
Compulsory Education &
Training, Edge Hill University

Very special thanks to John Clarke whose wisdom and insights have influenced the shape of this book.

Throughout my career, in order to be the best teacher that I can be, I have found it necessary to make time for both personal reflection on my own practice and as a result of this, identifying strengths and areas for development. Through this continuous process of reflection and development I never stop learning. Being a brilliant teacher is about being passionate about teaching and learning.

Kathryn Carman, Senior Lecturer,
Edge Hill University

Thanks to Felicity Watts and Kristin Susser for their professionalism. My sincere thanks go to Rhiannon Findlay and Helen Pritt at Routledge for their patience and support.

To me a brilliant teacher is a teacher who delivers lessons she/ he would like to see delivered to her/his children/family. Brilliant teaching is about striving for excellence whilst not forgetting to care.

Mrs Josette Arnold, Assistant Principal &
Specialist Leader of Education
Huyton Arts and
Sports Centre for Learning

Introduction

The aim of this book is to provide a rich source of creativity, ideas and real case studies on how to be a brilliant teacher in the classroom, lecture hall, workshop, salon, fire station and studio in your subject specialism which may span from A level mathematics, business, construction to hairdressing. I recognise the diversity of the sector and the learners and hope this book will inspire, motivate and empower you on your journey into and through your teaching career.

This book is aimed specifically at practitioners working in the Lifelong Learning Sector (LLS), including those teaching learners aged 14 plus in schools and colleges, those teaching adults in community learning venues and those working with undergraduate and postgraduate students in further and higher education institutions. As well as new and more experienced practitioners, I hope this book will prove useful for teachers-in-training to develop their knowledge, skills and practices and to embrace new opportunities to deliver truly outstanding and engaging teaching and learning.

This book may be read from cover to cover, in one sitting, or it may be read on a chapter-by-chapter basis over a longer period of time. Each chapter is designed so that it can be read in isolation, as and when needed, although references to topics covered in other chapters will be found from time to time.

Within each chapter, the reader will find a number of features that are designed to engage and inspire the reader, including provoking reflection and active response to the ideas and themes that are covered. These activities have been designed to facilitate practical application and great learning and teaching. The case studies and real-life examples that are to be found in this book are drawn from a variety of different teaching and training contexts, as examples of great teaching and reflection of the diversity of the learning and skills sector as a whole. A small number of sources, books, journal articles and websites, are recommended. These lists are by no means exhaustive: featured items have been chosen because of their suitability and value for use and study by trainee teachers in the learning and skills sector.

E-resources are available at: http://www.routledge.com/books/details/9780415519021/

Chapter 1

Learning and teaching for young people and adults

Chapter objectives

This chapter provides an overview of what the secondary (14 plus) and Lifelong Learning Sector (LLS) involves and offers an outline of the role of a professional lecturer/trainer in this area. It also discusses what it is to be a professional, offering an important account of professional learning. To support this it considers Reflection and Practice and Criticality and Theory.

So what do we mean by a Further Education (FE) teacher?

Further and Adult Education has a long history and is often traced back to the mediaeval guilds where elements of the vocabulary we still use (apprenticeship, for example) originated. The sector has always had a complicated relationship with other sectors because we have a strong tendency to associate education with children, so there seems to be something odd about adults in classrooms, doing homework or taking tests.

A part of this has been the way in which post-compulsory education has often been ignored or given a lesser status when governments have developed policy. Many major reforms and enquiries have treated education as being about schools with youngsters and adults being left out of the picture or mentioned as an afterthought. This gave the sector the image of being a 'poor cousin' for much of the last century, despite the fact that FE colleges, Adult Education Centres and other providers fulfilled a vital role in vocational and community education as well as holding out the possibility of a second chance to hundreds of thousands of people who had failed in or been failed by their school experience.

This semi-invisible quality extended to thinking about the people who taught in the sector. Most professions and crafts have a tradition whereby people who get on well in the job are encouraged to move into the preparation of the next generation of practitioners. This can also be seen as something which derives from the mediaeval guild model of master/journeyman/apprentice. On this model the FE teacher is often seen as a specialist who has 'paid her or his dues' within their job, has appropriate qualifications and experience and now wants to pass this on to others.

A parallel process can be identified in Adult Education where 'experts' of one sort or another (art, history, badminton. . . .yoga, zoology) wish to share that with other adults. By definition, this model usually involves people coming into the job later in life and it is usually thought to be inappropriate for initial training to follow on directly from full-time education. This also means that most FE and Adult Education (AE) teachers are 'dual professionals' who have qualifications and experience in their subject profession to which they want to add a new professional status as teachers.

So many lecturers in accountancy or bricklaying will answer when asked 'what do you do?', 'I am an accountant and I teach in the college, or I am a bricklayer and I work in the Training Centre'. This double identity is a valuable part of what makes the sector so rich and diverse but it can also cause problems for establishing the FE teacher as a clear professional category in its own right. This is compounded by the widespread view that all that really matters in teaching is good subject knowledge. Many (including the current secretary of state, apparently) hold the opinion that somebody who has fully mastered their subject will therefore be able to teach it effectively. This view is surprisingly widespread despite the fact that almost all of us have been taught by 'experts' who clearly knew their subject but were unable to organise it and present it in ways that engaged the learners in front of them.

This book is (unsurprisingly) committed to the idea that teaching is a skilled profession in its own right with its own body of knowledge and values and that while nobody would suggest trying to teach a subject without understanding it yourself, this is only the first step to being a competent, let alone a fantastic, FE teacher.

The term 'FE lecturer' in this book is used to indicate anyone working in the Lifelong Learning Sector (LLS), for example, teachers, tutors, trainers, mentors, assessors, managers and administrators. The post-compulsory education and training (PCET) sector is rightly celebrated for its richness in diversity. Teachers, trainers and tutors working in further education (FE) colleges, work-based learning (WBL) providers and organisations supporting community learning and development (CLD) as noted previously come from a variety of backgrounds, often entering teaching through non-traditional routes. Some of you may have gained your first experience of the post-compulsory sector as students in a College of Further Education and/or 6th form whilst gaining your subject specific qualifications. From that first step into the Lifelong Learning Sector (LLS) the drive for returning to the sector to teach will vary. A number of trainee teachers cite the reason being to emulate a teacher who has motivated and inspired them on their learning trajectory.

Reflection and activity

Being a great teacher means maintaining your occupational, specialist or subject knowledge. Feeling passionate about your specialised area can be contagious when you teach future generations of hairdressers, nurses, journalists, builders, horticulturists etc.

Activity
How do you maintain your specialist knowledge?

How do you maintain your passion for your specialised area and teaching?

When reading through text books on teaching and learning, 'passion' is often overlooked in favour of in-depth coverage of theories. Whilst theories have their place and will be explored in this book, I want to emphasise early that passion remains a vital part of being a great teacher.

The FE sector

The further education and skills sector has faced and continues to face an extraordinary level of change, indeed this is the case for all public services. To provide a context, it is helpful to give an over-view of the recent changes and their implications for your role as a professional. With the 1992 Further and Higher Education Act came the incorporation of FE colleges and their removal from local authority control. This shift brought a greater drive in the direction of a market-led approach with the emphasis on offering appropri-ate programmes and courses to meet the demands of the market. With the advent of these policies and reforms the last decade has seen a rapid increase in the number of people attending FE colleges, particularly within the 16–18 age range. This has led to the delivery of subjects in colleges widening and learner cohorts becoming more diverse. So, FE encompasses full-time or part-time, academic or vocational, learning or training for those (traditionally) over the age of 16 in a number of college and community settings. Further Education has strong bonds with disadvantaged groups and com-munities. For example, FE can offer basic skills courses in literacy and numeracy for adult returnees. Below Marie McNamara (2007), a single mum of three children, who worked as a machinist in a local factory on leaving school at fifteen and returned to adult education in her 30s, tells her story:

> **Getting Better**
> I was dreading my first lesson.
> Would I be taught with kids?
> But I needn't have worried.
> They were nearly all adults.
>
> People like me,
> Who thought they were thick
> Because they couldn't read,
> Write or spell.
>
> After all,
> that's what most of us
> Have grown up believing.
>
> Together we started the journey
> Towards a better life
>
> Returning to education
> To learn to read and write

Was one of the most frightening things
I have done,
But it was also one of the best.

(Ibid. 6–13)

Marie progressed from a basic skills course to an access to Higher
Education programme and then on to university to study nursing.
She is now a staff nurse in a hospital in the north-west of England.
Education had a powerful impact on her and her family's life
and the choices she/they were able to make. These stories and
bonds made with FE are strengths which enrich and empower communities and the lives of people within them. For example, most
colleges have outreach centres which offer links to other services
such as libraries and community centres. These more intimate settings can often be more suitable to the needs of those learners who
find engaging with large institutions intimidating. These settings
can offer people second chances to engage with education which
can make a real difference to their lives and opportunities. Bynner
and Parsons (2006) showed the strong link between poor basic
skills and disadvantaged life courses. In their report the results
show a disturbing picture of limited life chances, quality of life and
social inclusion between participants at or below Entry Level 2
compared with others at higher levels of literacy and numeracy
competence. Entry Level 2 skills were associated with lack of qualifications, poor employment experience and prospects, poor material and financial circumstances, poor health prospects and lack of
social and political participation. These were particularly notice-
able for adults whose skills were at Entry 2 or below. However, the
notion of their lives being determined by poverty and exclusion can
be challenged by returning to education where they are valued and
they can flourish to reach their potential.

Together with teaching adults, the drive for a collaborative
approach between colleges and schools placed the New Diploma at
its heart along with a move towards 14–16-year-olds being taught
in FE colleges by FE staff. Colleges have also made a concerted
effort to rebuild their involvement in apprenticeships in response
to the promotion of a reinvented apprenticeship system by New
Labour and the most recent Coalition government, most vocational
provision in FE remaining college- and not employer-situated, with
only 6 per cent of 16–18-year-olds in FE on apprenticeships in
2010/11 (AoC 2011a: 2).

There will be further changes to the make-up of FE colleges with the opportunity for them to set up their own '14 to 16 centres'. The new centres will aim to offer a combination of high quality vocational and academic subjects and aim to attract students of all abilities who want early access to practical and technical education. The decision is a response to the recommendation from Professor Alison Wolf in her review of vocational education (see Chapter 2). Professor Wolf found that for some young people, following a vocational route at 14 resulted in them doing better in the core academic subjects as well. She felt that an FE college, with its links to employers, workshops and equipment, can be the greatest place to do that.

Reflection and activity

Consider how your subject area can empower learners to move forward in their personal and/or professional life.

So, what does it mean to say that FE teachers are or should be professionals?

The popular view of professions is mixed. We use phrases like 'professional foul' to suggest that professions may well pass on cynical or self-serving values, and professions are often seen, as in George Bernard Shaw's words, as 'a conspiracy against the laity'. We can identify professional status with a kind of closed shop which protects the lifestyles of its own members. At the same time, the last hundred years have seen a general tendency for jobs of all kinds to try to attain professional status, a process sometimes called the 'professionalisation of everyone'. This process is driven by a mercenary sense that professions are better paid and better able to protect their rewards than non-professions and a desire to be part of what is still seen as a status group causing deference and respect among others, although this special status can be seen as declining.

A second concern is to develop professional standards and values, perhaps enforced by a professional body which lays down what kinds of knowledge and skills a practitioner should have and sets the rules by which they practise.

Jobs like nursing, librarianship, social work, personnel managers, etc., adopted a strategy of 'professionalisation'. This involved specifying acceptable levels of qualification, setting out and enforcing ethical codes, insisting on updating and staff development throughout people's careers, etc. Teaching could be seen as a *professionalising* occupation in this sense, with the process culminating in the establishment of the General Teaching Council in the 1990s. A similar process occurred in relation to FE teaching with a range of changes and initiatives which were seen by many as establishing professional status.

The last government supported professional values in FE by legislating for the registration of practitioners by the Institute for Learning (IfL), on the model of the General Medical Council or the General Council of the Bar, its historical genesis being a Victorian creation. All staff employed as teachers in the LLS sector were required to be professionally registered and all new staff were also required to be licensed to practise by the Institute for Learning (IfL). As described above, to be licensed, all teachers needed to be trained to a standard that allowed them to achieve either Qualified Teacher Learning and Skills (QTLS) status or Associate Teacher Learning and Skills (ATLS) status, depending on their role. All full-time teachers, which included new and existing teachers, needed to undertake at least 30 hours of Continued Professional Development (CPD) per year and keep a record reflecting on the CPD activities they have undertaken to maintain their status with the IfL.

Lord Lingfield's review of FE professionalism (2012) called for the IfL to become a voluntary body once again. The Lingfield report did not stop with the IfL in its changes to the 2007 regulations on FE teaching. It also proposed to up-end the entire system for teacher training in FE and make it possible for unqualified staff to work indefinitely in colleges and publicly funded training providers. The Lingfield review's recommendation to remove the legal requirement for staff to achieve teaching qualifications, which the sector has fought for in a bid to gain professional status, in favour of 'discretionary advice', seems at odds with its emphasis on quality and the professional status of teachers. The review proposes removing the lower-level 3 and 4 teaching qualifications and removing the naming system of PTLLS, CTLLS and DTLLS. There would remain a basic induction qualification, followed by a level 5 certificate in further education for most, with the option of a master's-level diploma for those deemed as elite teachers.

Education and Training Foundation

Further education Minister Mathew Hancock announced in October 2012 that the Association of Colleges (AoC) and the Association of Employment and Learning Providers (AELP) had won government approval to 'take forward' proposals for the FE Guild (Hancock 2012). The proposed function of the Guild included setting professional standards and codes of behaviour for members, developing qualifications for those working in the sector, and supporting training and strategic planning. However, on the 29th of May 2013, it was revealed that the FE Guild was to be known as the Education and Training Foundation and to be the new employer-led organisation for the sector. Time will tell how this pans out and what impact it has on the practitioner, learner and the sector as a whole.

So what is a profession?

It is surrounded (and perhaps engulfed) in a rapid wave of change that we consider with deeper criticality below: what is a profession?
Millerson identifies six 'most frequently mentioned' traits:

1. skill based on theoretical knowledge
2. the provision of training and education
3. testing the competence of members
4. organisation
5. adherence to a professional code of conduct
6. altruistic service.

(Millerson 1964)

It can be argued that the model rests on the idea of a 'true' profession, some kind of 'classic' example (medicine and law most often cited) and that this model describes what ought to be the case for others. Also simply listing traits allows claimants to emphasise or ignore traits that do not fit the case they are making. So people who wish to open up more occupations to professional status will opt for fewer traits more liberally defined, while those aiming to close off this option will opt for more numerous traits more strictly interpreted and may consequently wish to relegate claimant occupations to a subordinate category such as *semi-profession* (Etzioni 1969). More recently some authors have used the word in the sense of creating a professional standard of work or meeting agreed expectations, something that may be achieved by bureaucratic means or 'organisational professionalism' as well as by 'occupational professionalism' (Evetts 2009). Dominant models of professionalisation have their origins in the industrialisation and bureaucratisation of the twentieth and late nineteenth centuries, and are based in a 'technical-rational' or 'technocratic' way of thinking (Schön 1983, Bines 1992). This model gives priority to scientific values and ways of operating, and takes a technical and operational view of the education and role of the professional.

Debates about the attainment of professional status need to be set in a context of changing social attitudes and values. Partly as a result of the cynical view of professions discussed above and partly because of the New Right's political hostility to what they saw as 'restrictive practices', hostile to the unfettered power of the marketplace and client/consumer sovereignty, the period since the 1970s has seen a decline in popular deference towards professions (Eraut 1994, p. 5). There has grown up a generalised scepticism towards 'expert knowledge' and 'professional bodies' capacity or willingness to protect the public, which is reflected in many areas such as the reaction to GM foods, the Harold Shipman case or the recent economic crash, seen as being caused by professional bankers and economists. We are perhaps in an ironic situation that a large number of occupations are pursuing a goal of professionalisation which is itself being steadily emptied of its political and social significance by broader social changes.

Professional work

One final area of recent debate which needs to be addressed before discussing Further Education teaching is the nature of professional work. What is it about the nature of work practices themselves which qualifies them as being professional? Are there characteristics of some occupations which make a claim to status based on education and credentials more effective than others? This question obviously ties the notion of professionals' special status to the related idea that professions are characterised by mastery of 'professional bodies of knowledge'.

A number of writers have attempted to identify what it is which characterises professional work so as to inform attempts to assess and accredit professional training. Wilfred Carr (1995) argues that in the case of the teaching profession the nature of professionalism is a matter of moral judgement as much as of effectiveness of the relevant deployment of knowledge. Following a model taken from Aristotle's concept of 'Practical Wisdom' he argues that each profession is particularly concerned with the realisation of some aspect of 'the good life'. Lawyers are concerned with justice, doctors with physical well-being, and teachers with understanding. This makes professional practices inherently difficult as they are concerned with complex judgements and dilemmas. Moral judgements almost always involve the need to make decisions between competing moral claims, e.g. for a doctor between the demands of respect for a patient's privacy and the wish to involve family and friends in supporting them through an illness. Further, as Winter points out, professions have a moral imperative to avoid what he calls 'oppressive' judgements, i.e. those based on non-justifiable discriminations on the basis of age, gender, sexual orientation, race, etc.

> This value commitment is intrinsic to professional work because professional workers have an inherent responsibility to ensure that their services . . . are equally available to all members of society. This principle of equity as applied to all clients (often expressed in official 'ethical codes') means that professional workers' specific skills are particularly required by vulnerable (disadvantaged, oppressed) citizens, who thus provide the real test of the profession's effectiveness.
>
> (Winter 1993, p. 13)

Winter goes on to stress the extent to which the moral and inter-personal nature of professional practice entails a serious professional engagement with emotional aspects of life. '. . . [F]or professional workers emotions (their own as well as clients') are a topic, an obstacle and a resource' (ibid., p. 13).

Morality and emotion then are vital aspects of what might be seen as a more sophisticated model of professional work than the one which simply stresses a change towards 'more knowledge'. Nevertheless all the definitions of professionalism we examined earlier did stress knowledge as a vital aspect, so what is the specific role of knowledge in professional practice?

Dreyfus and Dreyfus discussed the question of the role of knowledge from the point of view of the role of artificial intelligence in decision making. They challenged what has become known as the 'Expert Systems' model. This view is based on the idea that all decision making is based on the application of knowledge in a systematic and structured way to problems. Knowledge is seen as a series of propositional statements which can be codified and organised in the kind of systematic formats used by computers. Notionally then computers could be designed to make the kind of 'knowledge-informed' decisions which we see as traditionally the preserve of experts in general and professionals in particular.

The Dreyfuses reject this view. They argue that professional work is typified by relatively 'unstructured' situations. Where some manufacturing processes such as 'blending petroleum' might be amenable to the kind of systematic application of knowledge to decisions suggested above, most human interactions, whether educational, caring or commercial, are not. The systems (rules of thumb, tips for teachers etc.) act as props for a period while the newcomer develops the kinds of experience and perception which will enable them to make decisions without reference to them. The expert develops *tacit understandings* and intuitive judgement. (For an application of this model to nursing see Benner 1984.) 'At the highest level of skill ... understanding is created unconsciously from concrete experience and cannot be verbalised' (Dreyfus 1981, p. 38).

This critique of formal analytical models of practice has the great strength of seeing knowledge as less abstract and more 'situational' than might be suggested by the advocates of computer modelling, but it leads to problems when it stresses the unspoken intuitive nature of professional expertise. If professional expertise cannot be reconstructed outside the consciousness of the experienced practitioner, then how can it be subjected to critique and how can it be passed on from professional to professional in any kind of systematic way? What is there to prevent professional expertise becoming the basis for a self-justifying personal or group ideology? 'I just know these things from experience. I cannot explain it so you cannot learn it or criticise it.'

Reflection and activity

Janet Lord, a teacher educator, lecturer and consultant in Psychology and Education, shares the case study of John and issues affecting professional identity for teachers starting off in the lifelong learning sector.

When reading Janet's case study consider the issues which affect or have the potential to affect your professional identity.

Janet Lord: Case study

What do I think, feel and do as a teacher in the lifelong learning sector? This question is linked inextricably to ideas of agency and action and to professional identity.

Professional identity is a rather nebulous concept to define, but perhaps it should be seen as a process rather than as a single, fixed outcome. James Gee (2001) suggests that there are four ways of thinking about identity which may help us as we try and work out what professional identity is about:

- Nature identity refers to the bits of identity which we are born with, like our gender.
- Institutional identity is the identity conferred upon us by an institution, such as by a college when we get a teaching job, or when we get our QTLS certificate.
- Discourse identity is that identity which is developed through discourses with other people; so for example, a teacher might become known as the 'organised one' or the 'lively one' and this identity is developed through discourses and interactions with other individuals.
- Affiliative identity is developed through membership of a group, such as a group of NQTs in college, or a group of PE teachers, or another such community of practice.

The case study of John will be used to illustrate what kind of factors may influence the development of professional identity of teachers in the lifelong learning sector.

John is a male teacher trainee nearing the end of his course at a local university with an excellent reputation for ITE. He is currently on placement at an FE college in a deprived area, an area where well over two-thirds of school children are entitled to free school meals. He is a mature student, who joined teaching after a successful career as a chemist in the local industrial laboratories. In these laboratories most of the research staff were male and the administrative staff female. The changes to PGCE bursaries mean that

John is having to supplement his income with part-time work. He passed all his ITE skills tests at university within a few weeks of starting the course. The FE college he is at is considering entering into a partnership with the nearest HEI and providing foundation degrees. The principal of the college is ambitious. John's mentor, the head of science, is an older woman who has been at the college many years. John enjoys his work and sees himself as a Vygotskian, providing a supportive environment in which he can facilitate peer-assisted learning. However, to his surprise he has had some problems with behaviour management with the students in his classes.

The most important thing that this example shows is that what John is experiencing in his placement is the result of a dynamic interaction of a whole set of factors.

Some of these are quite distant from John as an individual. Such factors are likely to be more related to structural influences on John than to his own subjectively-oriented understandings; one such factor might be the perceived status of teachers in society, which is known to change over time (e.g. Zembylas 2003) and of men in the teaching profession (Gee 2001). Such circumstances will form part of a mix of factors which may impact on the development of John's professional identity. Also in this mix are current government policies and initiatives, such as the cuts to PGCE bursary funding, which have meant John has to work part-time as well as study, and which may well have affected his motivation for his training. The emphasis on skills-testing for teachers (Department for Education 2011) is also likely to be a key influence on John's professional identity; the initial emphasis on skills in his ITE course may well be evident throughout John's career. The location of John's college placement in a deprived area may have an impact on his professional identity and may determine his attitude to his job, his learners and the interactions between the education system and other systems such as health and social welfare.

Other factors are more immediately relevant to John – for example, factors such as the culture of John's college. An FE college looking for a partnership with a university is likely to engender a different culture and hence set of professional identities than, say a small sixth form college. Some of the characteristics of John's mentor as an experienced head of science, with her own pedagogic preferences and style, will also fit in here, as will the management style and philosophy of education of the college leaders – these may impact on their expectations of John and his agency and effectiveness.

The discourses in which John engages are key; some of the main stakeholders in these discourses are the learners and the staff with whom John interacts on a regular basis, and so his professional identity may to a large extent be defined by these individuals.

At a much more personal level, John brings his own personality and his individual characteristics to the mix, for example, his previous background and the professional identity he developed on his earlier career path. Coming from a career in the chemical industry may mean that he puts a strong emphasis on health and safety issues in his teaching. The genderised environment where he was working may have an impact on his attitudes to learners – he may have to challenge his own stereotypical ideas about the nature of suitable careers for males and females, for example. John's Vygotskian educational philosophy, with its emphasis on the social factors relating to learning, in combination with his relative inexperience, may be one of the sources which contributes to his behaviour management problems. This will inevitably have an impact on how he interacts with his students, and hence on his developing sense of agency and identity.

John's own educational background, male gender and his personal circumstances will also impact on the development of his professional identity, as these factors interact with the others which may affect him.

We can see from this case study that there is a fast-changing dynamism, a fluid and facilitating intersectionality about how a range of factors may affect the development of John's professional identity. By 'intersectionality' I mean that various biological, social and cultural factors interact on multiple and often simultaneous levels.

The case of John demonstrates the dynamic intersectionality of the factors which may impact on the development of the professional identity of a teacher in the lifelong learning sector. At the same time, early career teachers such as John are situated and situating themselves in the immediate and lived reality of particular teaching and learning contexts, and they are working through ideas of affinity with other trainees and teachers with whom they interact.

My argument is that these reflexive and reflective processes are important in the creation of a professional identity. An understanding of the factors which may mediate the development of teachers' professional identity may have a key effect on the development of their agency and actions as teachers in the lifelong learning sector.

Professional learning

What the model of intuitive understanding, discussed earlier, leaves out of account then is any model of how professionals actually learn. They seem to simply 'come to be' professional by some kind of action-based osmosis. There is a stress on the necessary role of experience but little description of how this experience converts into knowledge or expertise.

One classic exposition of this process is the model of learning from experience proposed by David Kolb (Kolb 1984; Gibbs 1988). This model is based on the idea of learning as a cyclical process where the learner moves from concrete experiences through reflection, conceptualisation and experiment to new experiences understood in the light of changed perceptions. At the heart of this model is the one element which might be seen as crucial to professionalism – that of reflection. We will discuss this model of learning in a later chapter. Meanwhile it is worth noting as this idea is at the heart of the work of the key figure in thinking about professional learning in the last decade, Donald Schön.

Schön's key concern is to describe the nature of the learning processes which take place within professional practice. Like the work of the Dreyfuses, Schön's writings are based on his rejection of what he saw as the dominant model of professional knowledge based on 'technical rationality'. This means that Schön has a very specific notion of the kind of work which can be identified as professional. Indeed his hostility to 'technical rationality' might seem to suggest that occupations without a human or creative dimension might be seen as by definition non-professional. Schön attempts to construct an '. . . epistemology of practice implicit in the artistic intuitive processes which some practitioners do bring to situations of uncertainty, instability, uniqueness and value conflict' (Schön 1983, p. 49).

His approach is based on the idea of the indeterminacy of significant areas of professional practice. He sees professionals as commonly engaging in complex and ill-defined situations which require creative and original responses if a solution is to be found. In these unpredictable situations professionals draw on their experiences as if intuitively (knowing-in-action) but at the same time they *reflect* on what it is they are doing. It is this latter aspect that Schön stresses. Dreyfus among others had emphasised the role of the apparently intuitive in professional decision making. Schön adds the idea of 'reflection-in-action'.

Reflection is triggered for the professional when situations appear not to be normal and require some kind of special attention. Situations come to be seen as problematic because of something unusual or something which does not work.

Schön on Reflection

Routine responses produce a surprise – an unexpected outcome, pleasant or unpleasant, that does not fit the categories of our knowing-in-action.

- Surprise leads to reflection within an action-present. Reflection is at least in some measure conscious, although it need not occur in the medium of words. We consider both the unexpected event and the knowing-in-action which led up to it, asking ourselves, as it were, 'What is this?' and at the same time, 'How have I been thinking about this?'. Our thought turns back on the surprising phenomenon and at the same time back on itself.
- Reflection-in-action has a critical function, questioning the assumptional structure of knowing-in-action. We think critically about the thinking that got us into this fix or this opportunity: and we may, in the process restructure strategies of action, understandings of phenomena, or ways of framing problems. . . .
- Reflection gives rise to on-the-spot experiment. We think up and try out new actions intended to explore the newly observed phenomena, test our tentative understandings of them or affirm the moves we have invented to change things for the better . . . On the spot experiment may work, again in the sense of yielding intended results or it may produce surprises that call for further reflection and experiment.
- The description I have given is, of course an idealised one. The moments of reflection-in-action are rarely as distinct from one another as I have made them out to be.

The experience of surprise may present itself in such a way as to seem already interpreted, the criticism and restructuring of knowing-in-action may be compressed into a single process. But regardless of the distinctness of its moments or the constancy of their sequence, what distinguishes reflection-in-action from other kinds of reflection is its immediate significance for action.

(Schön 1987, pp. 28–29)

This notion of reflection-in-action has been phenomenally successful in terms of its influence over professional educators. 'The Reflective Practitioner has probably been the most quoted book of professional expertise during the last ten years' (Eraut 1994, p. 142). It also coincided with the growth of a concern with the need to define professionalism in the curricula of 'newly professionalising' occupations (Goodlad 1984; Becher 1994; Troman 2007).

Nevertheless it has evoked a range of critiques which tend to emphasise the problematic nature of Schön's concept of reflection. Winter points out that Schön's work is not actually derived from studies of professionals' own practice. Rather it is based on 'sessions where experienced practitioners in a tutorial role are attempting to pass on their knowledge to novices. But . . . we will not be surprised to learn that there is evidence that experts do not actually follow (in practice) the instructions they use in instructing trainees!' (Winter 1993, p. 17).

Wellington and Austin point out that the idea of the reflective practitioner is actually reinterpreted by professionals in very different ways, reflecting a range of different emphases and models of professional good practice (Wellington and Austin 1996). Eraut's critique goes further than these in questioning the value of the concept of reflection in Schön's work. Instead he proposes a model which is based on a more subtle understanding of the role of time in distinguishing between the kinds of immediate adjustments made during practice and the sorts of deliberation and conceptual re-thinking which may be pursued later. He wishes to describe Schön's idea of rapid reflection-in-action as a form of 'meta-cognition during skilled behaviour', while the kind of re-framing and reflective conversation Schön goes on to describe are seen by Eraut as further levels of meta-cognition (Eraut 1994, p. 14).

Summarising professionalism

Despite these critiques there emerges from the above descriptions a set of key ideas about the nature of professional work which can inform discussions of claims to professionalism and professional training. These key ideas are:

a) Professional work involves situations which are unique and indeterminate. These situations are not susceptible to the application of neat formulae.
b) Practice changes understanding and understanding changes practice. This involves a process of reflection. This reflection will focus on the similarities and differences between different clients (students) and situations. It will involve critical and analytical thought.
c) While professional workers have access to a range of information relevant to their role, its application to individual cases will depend on what Winter calls their 'own resourceful interpretation'.
d) Professional work has a central *ethical* dimension which requires practitioners to apply moral judgements and take moral responsibilities for their actions. This commitment includes a commitment to behaviour which is based on an equal respect for the needs of all clients and potential clients.
e) Professional work has an *emotional* dimension which involves responsibilities in relation to their own feelings as well as those of clients (students). Self-knowledge and knowledge of others play a major part in this.
f) The indeterminacy and unpredictability of professional practice necessitates a commitment to the *provisional and incomplete nature of judgements and knowledge* – the openness to reflection and feedback from peers and clients.

How far does this work help to clarify the debates about claims to professional status for FE teachers outlined above?

The stress on the peculiarly context-specific nature of professional knowledge obviously serves some groups in their resistance to views of their role which would routinise and control their practice. The idea of 'reflective practice' has been seen in teacher education as a 'red rag to the Ofsted bull' when institutions have been faced with the need to justify their practice in inspections. Clearly some critics see the model as preventing the development of a centrally prescribed, appropriately effective 'evidence-based practice' (Hargreaves 1996).

Duckworth and Tummons (2010) whilst acknowledging the limitations of reflective practice also highlight the strengths of learning from experience through critical reflection (experiential learning). Ingle and Duckworth (2013) propose an interpretation of the reflective process with the 'Independent Reflective Investigation for Solution(s)' model (IRIS). The IRIS lens of reflection encourages a solutions-based approach to addressing barriers or concerns in professional practice. Four sequential lenses are presented to guide reflectors to consider how their existing strengths and on-going skills development can be used to identify an intervention. The model encourages practitioners to move through the flow of reflection, focusing on how interventions may be implemented practically and what impact they may have on both future practice and learning outcomes. For a number of teachers the best part of teaching is the learning and growth they get from it and reflection can facilitate this in expected and unexpected ways. This in turn can have a deep impact which challenges and changes their previously held values, beliefs and assumptions.

Final thoughts . . .

While the goal of effective teaching and learning can be seen as shared by the interests of markets and bureaucracies as well as professionals, there are tensions between on the one hand the sector's professionalisation agenda and on the other the target-driven and contractually-based reforms that are also driving change. It is amongst these tensions that as teachers we navigate. The intangibility and indeterminacy of the professional knowledge base may serve to strengthen arguments for autonomy but it can also be seen as reinforcing public and official doubts about the special status of professionals.

Further reading

Ball, S. (2008), *The Education Debate*. Bristol: The Policy Press.

Coffield, F., S. Edward, I. Finlay, A. Hodgson, K. Spours, R. Steer and M. Gregson (2007), 'How policy impacts on practice and how practice does not impact on policy,' *British Educational Research Journal* 33 (5), 723–741.

Duckworth, V. & J. Tummons (2010), *Current Issues in Lifelong Learning*. Maidenhead: Open University Press.

Websites

Learning and Skills Improvement Service: http://tlp.excellencegateway.org.uk/teachingandlearning/downloads/index_lsis.html

Department for Education: http://www.education.gov.uk/childrenandyoungpeople/youngpeople/qandlearning/a00202523/reform-of-14-to-16-performance-tablesepartment for Education

National Research Development Centre for Adult Literacy and Numeracy: http://www.nrdc.org.uk/

Chapter 2

Recent policy in the Lifelong Learning Sector

Chapter objectives

This chapter provides an overview of the recent policy change in the Lifelong Learning Sector. To support this it considers legislation funding and structures. It also considers changes to approaches to learning – pedagogy and andragogy and treating our learners as adults.

Introduction

Post-Compulsory Education and Training (PCET) has been significantly reshaped by national policy initiatives since the 1970s when the government took a bigger interest in the education and training of adults, as the concept of lifelong learning fed into international policy documents (Field 2000). The impact of policy can occasionally be difficult for practitioners to appreciate fully. The environment of the classroom can seem very separate from the governmental departments that work at local, national and indeed International level. The actions, motives and language of politics are often very unlike the kinds of issues, agendas, activities or decisions that we are normally involved with on a day to day basis. Indeed, as busy teachers our minds and actions are often very much on keeping abreast of what we need to do for our next lesson and group of learners. And whilst decisions about funding or qualifications reform are of importance to classroom practitioners and their practice, the effects of policy shifts can sometimes take time to filter down to grassroots level and can be a shock when it impacts on the way practitioners can operate in their classroom practice and indeed are perceived as professionals (for example, consider the debate on professionalism and changing reforms in Chapter 1).

Policy change

Over ten years ago, *The Learning Age* document supported Britain's drive for business and commerce, noting that: 'Learning will be the key to a strong economy and an inclusive society' (DfEE 1998: 3). Four years later, another key government policy document, *Success for All,* stated how the government's goals should be 'social inclusion and economic prosperity' (DfES 2002: 9). The rhetoric being used in the policies and reports may be viewed as corresponding to an instrumental model with a drive towards employability in the labour market as the key to social inclusion. With this in mind, employability has acquired a central role within policy, strategy and the student curriculum.

Reflection and activity

Consider the driving factors of your curriculum.

Green Paper: 'Every Child Matters', 2003

The Green Paper was drafted to coincide with a response to the findings of Lord Laming's report into the death of Victoria Climbié and a report by the Social Exclusion Unit regarding raising the educational attainment of looked-after children. Its purpose is to propose improvements and changes to support children, young people and their families, particularly within child protection services.

Prior to writing the Green Paper the government consulted with a range of children, young people and families, who identified five outcomes which mattered most to them and that they felt were key to well-being in childhood and later life. These were:

- *Being healthy* – enjoying good physical and mental health and living a healthy lifestyle
- *Staying safe* – being protected from harm and neglect
- *Enjoying and achieving* – getting the most out of life and developing the skills for adulthood
- *Making a positive contribution* – being involved with the community and society and not engaging in anti-social or offending behaviour

- *Economic well-being* – not being prevented by economic disadvantage from achieving their full potential.

The coalition government has distanced itself from the rhetoric of
what we called the Every Child Matters (EC(L)M) agenda; a host
of new policies is now occupying the ideological forefront.
How the principles and structures of EC(L)M will continue is as
yet unclear.

'Equipping our Teachers for the Future' (DfES), 2004

This publication set out a commitment to revise the 2001 regulations
(FENTO standards), supported by new professional standards and
a Teacher Qualifications Framework of new teaching qualification
routes. These reforms (implementation date, September 2007)
included the introduction of:

- Preparing to Teach in the Lifelong Learning Sector (PTLLS)
  minimum threshold licence to teach for all teachers, trainers
  and tutors
- Certificate in Teaching in the Lifelong Learning Sector (or HEI
  equivalent) for those in an Associate teaching role, leading to
  Associate Teacher Learning and Skills status (ATLS)
- Diploma in Teaching in the Lifelong Learning Sector (or HEI
  equivalent) at minimum Level 5 leading to Qualified Teacher
  Learning and Skills (QTLS) status for those in a full teaching role.

White Paper: '14–19 Education and Skills' (DfES), 2005

Historically, there have been a number of changes to the A Level
system in England and Wales since it was introduced in 1949. In
February 2005, Ruth Kelly (the then new Secretary of State for
Education) produced a government White Paper outlining plans for
14–19 Education. The White Paper *14–19 Education and Skills*
(DfES 2005) rejected the main Tomlinson recommendation for a
unified multi-level diploma system. Instead, it proposed the development of Diplomas available in a range of 14 industry/employ-
ment sectors. These are known as lines of learning to provide a
ladder of progression of broad vocational qualifications throughout

the 14–19 phase, together with modifications to GCSE and A Level specifications. The new qualifications formed the apex of the first ever statutory 14–19 National Entitlement for learners, aimed at providing both breadth and choice of study and institutional setting. It meant the LLS could deliver to 14–16-year-olds. It also identified the need for more work-based learning trajectories and strategies to engage the disaffected and low attaining students in mainstream schools which included personalised programmes, a flexible approach, an increased development of personal and social skills and an emphasis on functional skills.

The Foster Report 'Realising the Potential: A Review of the Future Role of Further Education Colleges', 2005

Published on 15th November, the review argued that there was a need for a clearly recognised and shared key purpose and drive among FE colleges that focuses on the needs of both learners and business. The 2005 Foster Review and 2006 Leitch Review defined 'quality' as matching provision to local labour market and employer needs. Both reports urged the Learning and Skills Council (LSC) to introduce greater competition in the sector and only purchase provision that employers wanted.

White Paper: 'Raising Skills, Improving Life Chances' (DfES), 2006

This White Paper builds on the existing 14–19 Education and Skills White Paper and Skills Strategy to set out a series of FE reforms making the FE system fit for purpose in meeting the two strategic challenges of transforming 14–19 education and up-skilling the adult workforce. It sets out major reform for colleges and training providers, building on the recommendations of the Foster Review.

Leitch review of skills 'Prosperity for All in the Global Economy', 2006

The Leitch Review was launched due to concerns over the ability of the UK to compete in increasingly globalised markets. According to Leitch, the UK suffered serious deficiencies in skills compared to other developed economies and needed an urgent programme to correct this comparative disadvantage. The report makes clear that in a rapidly changing global economy, with emerging economies such as India and China growing dramatically, the UK cannot afford to stand still. Despite having made good progress over the last decade, aspects of the UK's skills base remain weaker than those in other developed economies. The review set a number of ambitious targets for up-skilling the workforce, including 80 per cent of adults to have level 2 qualifications by 2010 and a 95 per cent rate of functional literacy and numeracy by 2020. The main recommendations of Leitch involved strengthening the demand-led nature of the UK vocational and education and training system.

Further Education Teachers' Qualifications (England) Regulations, 2007

Equipping our Teachers also proposed the establishment of a professional body for teachers and trainers in the lifelong learning sector. Consequently, the Institute for Learning (IfL) was established in 2007, with the aim of representing the collective interests of this varied group of professionals. It served to provide professional recognition for practitioners, through the monitoring and awarding of QTLS/ATLS status for teachers. Continuing professional development (CPD), a mandatory requirement for full-time and part-time teachers, continues to provide the mechanism through which QTLS/ATLS status is conferred and falls under the purview of the IfL.

Education and Skills Act, 2008

The Education and Skills Act 2008 set out that from 2015 all 16- and 17-year-olds will be required to participate in education or training. The eligible forms of education or training for young people to participate in are:

1. appropriate full-time education or training;
2. a contract of apprenticeship; or
3. part-time education or training towards an accredited qualification as part of full-time occupation or alongside occupation of more than 20 hours a week.

Review of the Vocational Education, The Wolf Report (DfE, 2011)

In September 2010 the Secretary of State for Education (Michael Gove) commissioned Professor Alison Wolf of King's College London to carry out an independent review of vocational education. Professor Wolf was asked to consider how vocational education for 14- to 19-year-olds could be improved in order to promote successful progression into the labour market and into higher level education and training routes. She was also asked to provide practical recommendations to help inform future policy direction, taking into account current financial constraints.

In March 2011 Professor Wolf presented her report and identified how in the lack of a formal definition, the term 'vocational' is not clearly defined by the education community. Vocational education, and its associated range of qualifications, serves many different purposes and many different learners, from diverse backgrounds and across levels. The report identified a number of key findings:

- Around two and a half million young people in England are aged 14 to 19, the vast majority of whom are engaged full or part-time in education.
- Vocational education includes courses and programmes which teach important and valuable skills to a very high standard. It offers a direct route into higher education and prestigious apprenticeships.
- Most English young people now take some vocational courses before they are 16 and post-16 the majority follow courses which are largely or entirely vocational.
- Many 16- and 17-year-olds move in and out of education and short-term employment.
- Between a quarter and a third of the post-16 cohort take low-level vocational qualifications, most of which have little to no labour market value.
- Among 16- to 19-year-olds, the Review estimates that at least 350,000 get little to no benefit from the post-16 education system.
- Less than 50% of students have both English and Maths GCSE (at grades A*-C) at the end of Key Stage 4 (age 15/16) and at age 18 the figure is still below 50%. Only 4% of the cohort achieve this during their 16–18 education.

Twenty-seven recommendations were made which included changes to funding and accountability, core curriculum requirements, and changes in the way qualifications are developed and regulated. Following this, in May 2011 the Government published its response to Professor Wolf's recommendations. The Government accepted all of the recommendations and set out its strategy for how the recommendations would be taken forward.

The Department for Education notes the key recommendations as:

- incentivising young people to take the most valuable vocational qualifications pre-16, while removing incentives to take large numbers of vocational qualifications to the detriment of core academic study;
- introducing principles to guide study programmes for young people on vocational routes post-16 to ensure they are gaining skills which will lead to progression into a variety of jobs or further learning, in particular to ensure that those who have not secured a good pass in English and maths GCSE continue to study those subjects;
- evaluating the delivery structure and content of apprenticeships to ensure they deliver the right skills for the workplace;
- making sure the regulatory framework moves quickly away from accrediting individual qualifications to regulating awarding organisations;
- removing the requirement that all qualifications offered to 14- to 19-year-olds fit within the Qualifications and Credit Framework (QCF), which has had a detrimental effect on their appropriateness and has left gaps in the market;
- enabling FE lecturers and professionals to teach in schools, ensuring young people are being taught by those best suited.

Lord Lingfield's review of FE professionalism, 2012

Following the publication of an interim report in March 2012, Lord Lingfield published his final report on professionalism in the Further Education workforce in October 2012. Working with an expert panel drawn from the sector, Lord Lingfield was commissioned by the Government to see how the Further Education sector can best serve its workforce, its students and the country. Their conclusions include:

- endorsement of the creation of a Further Education Guild which would set professional standards and establish a refreshed relationship between employers and staff;
- teachers of English and maths and those working with students with learning difficulties or disabilities should have specialist qualifications rather than relying on past qualifications or experiences.

There have also been changes regarding the strategic leadership for the sector. Whereas it had been assumed that LSIS might be the ones to take ownership of the sector, then speculation about it being the FE Guild, the main player is the Education and Training Foundation.

Reflection and activity

Read the following narrative and consider the impact of the changing nature of work, policy, ICT and lifelong learning on your learners' curriculum and working life.

Globalisation, competition and rapid progress of technology have also caused a shift in the nature and patterns of working life and employment. The current plans for the UK remain ambitious. In 2010, the UK commission stated:

It is our ambition to be one of the top countries in the world – for jobs, for productivity and for skills. A World Class economy, built on World Class skills, supporting World Class jobs and businesses. We should aim to be in the top quartile of OECD countries in all three – jobs, productivity and skills – by 2020. This means being in the top eight countries of the world. Our future prosperity depends ultimately on employment and productivity: how many people are in work and how productive they are when they are in work. Skills are essential to both.

If we are to become World Class, we must raise our game to match the productivity, skills and jobs of the best.

(ibid.: 6)

Due to shifts in working patterns of employment, many people do not have the same stability of employment or the same length of service with a single employer. The concept of a 'job for life' now seems a thing of the past to many people, many being displaced from traditional to new forms of work. A good example of this is in the implementation of ICT across many industrial sectors. Previously labour-intensive processes have been automated, with ICT changing the nature of work, speed and volume of communication, information and working practices. In 2008, a report by the Teaching and Learning Research Programme (TLRP) identified how the 'demand for knowledge workers rises exponentially in the knowledge economy [and] has resulted in a shift from mechanical Taylorism to digital Taylorism, so that knowledge work becomes portable working knowledge' (Brown 2008: 1). Under the premise of a 'knowledge economy' one of the most significant duties given to education is to provide a flexible, adaptable and skilled work-force to make countries competitive in the globalised economy.

Changes in legislation funding and structures

Further education colleges increasingly deal with a diverse and wide community of students: 14–16s; 16–19s; and over 19s. As such, they draw down funding from a variety of bodies (which themselves have gone through various models over recent years) that in turn are answerable to two different government departments that have quite specific responsibilities. Responsibility for funding post-16 learning in England is shared between the Department for Education (16–18-year-olds) and the Department for Business, Innovation and Skills (19-year-olds and over).

With Higher Education in Further Education (HE in FE) representing a significant component of the current Government's commitment to widening participation in HE, and with colleges working closely with businesses as part of Train to Gain, BIS is clearly an important stakeholder within the FE sector. Responsibility for students aged 14 to 19, however, rests with the Department for Children, Schools and Families (DCSF).

Soon after it came to power, the Coalition closed the YPLA and, in its place, a new Education Funding Agency (EFA) was established with a larger remit of funding three to 19 education. In 16 to 19 education, the reforms point in two quite different directions. On one hand, the Government will largely remove any role for central planning and fund providers on the basis of student demand and outcomes alone – specifically according to the number of students enrolled from the previous year and individual qualifications passed. Further education (FE) and sixth form colleges could be funded for 14- to 16-year-olds on a similar basis to schools from 2013.

Reflection and activity

Keeping abreast of the wider context, and recognising changes in the political, social and economic climate that impact on your learners' needs is essential to your role as a professional teacher.

Activity
Consider the implications of any recent policy changes on your learners' educational opportunities and/or experience in the classroom.

Adult learning, dialogue and personal development

The key feature of learning in our sector, and one that is often ignored, is that it is an **adult** learning process, i.e. it differs in a number of ways from the learning of school children.

Malcolm Knowles (1980, 1984) identifies a number of key characteristics of what he calls 'andragogy', a theory of adult learning. He argues among other things that adult learners are motivated by a developed sense of personal relevance in their approach to learning and have considerable stocks of previous experience to draw on in making sense of new experiences.

Knowles makes a clear distinction between adult and childhood learning. Indeed he attempted to popularise the word 'andragogy' (the art and science of helping adults learn) which was to be contrasted with *pedagogy* (the art and science of teaching children) as a way of highlighting the contrast.

Knowles claims there are four main principles which underlie the special character of adult learning:

1. Learning for adults involves changes in *self-concept*. Adults need to be more self-directive.
2. Learning for adults needs to be rooted in *previous experience* since adults bring with them a stock of experience which is a vital resource for the learning process.
3. Learning for adults needs to be clearly *relevant* to their interests and needs, as they have limited and contested time available.
4. Learning for adults need to be centred on *problems* rather than subjects. Adults are keen to apply and relate their learning to real situations.

These descriptions of adult learning are obviously open to debate and his strategy of contrasting adults with children (don't children have experiences, isn't their time valuable?) has drawn much criticism.

What Knowles' model does demonstrate is the way in which learning for adults is rarely something which can be easily compartmentalised and separated off from other aspects of life. If you have seen the film Educating Rita by Willy Russell, you will have noticed the way in which the central character is *transformed* in more ways than would be identified by the course brochure. This is not just the case for Open University degrees in English Literature!

Similarly there is a strong stress on autonomy and self-direction in Knowles' model. Knowles sees adults as people who are responsible for themselves and therefore he argues they should be encouraged to take responsibility for their own learning. This reflects the view of writers like Carl Rogers (1969) who argues that the key to an adult view of learning is 'freedom to learn'. Adults have an inbuilt potential for learning which the teacher should 'facilitate' rather than lead. The job of teachers is to engineer the circumstances where students can learn effectively for themselves.

What Knowles stresses is the need for an approach to adult learning which acknowledges the needs of the learner as an adult human being. This respects their experiences and their sense of relevance and allows them a major input into the planning and control of their learning.

Learning changes people and workplace learning changes workplaces. This is important to bear in mind when considering adults' learning.

Reflection and activity

Consider:

- How have you changed in your approach to learning since you were at school?
- The difficulties implicit in following Knowles' model. What are the downsides to 'autonomy and self-direction'?
- Is knowledge, skills or personal development most important to you and your role as a teacher?

Armitage et al. (2003) produced a useful chart comparing the assumptions of andragogy to those of pedagogy.

Table 2.1 The assumptions of andragogy

	Pedagogical	Andragogical
Concept of the learner	Dependent personality	Increasingly self-directed
Role of the learner's experience	To be built on more than used as a resource	A rich resource for learning by self and other
Reading to learn	Uniform by age, level and curriculum	Develops from life tasks and problems
Orientation to learning	Subject-centred	Task- or problem-centred
Motivation	By external rewards and punishment	By internal incentives and curiosity

Source: Armitage (2003: 79)

Important Note

Note that all models and frameworks are included to give you ideas and to start you thinking. Adapt or amend them if you have a different perspective. At the end of this book, the intention is that you will be able to think clearly for yourself about what makes learning effective and how to be as good as you can be at helping this to happen for your learners.

Reflection and activity

Angie Simms, ESOL Lecturer, Teaching and Learning Coach and Initial Teacher Trainer shares what makes an outstanding ESOL teacher. Consider how Angie's approaches could be used in your classroom.

I often ask learners on my initial teacher training course to look back at their educational experience and describe what makes a good teacher. They recall men and women who share a familiar range of desirable qualities. Good teachers, they say, need to be great communicators, well-organised, patient and conscientious, in control but with a strong sense of humour, knowledgeable and willing to go that extra mile. I would certainly agree with all of those attributes, but in my experience there are other, less obvious skills and abilities that an ESOL teacher must develop in order to be truly outstanding.

Perhaps the most important of these is empathy. Most of our learners are 'strangers in a strange land'. They come to us from a wide range of backgrounds and cultures, but all are struggling to make themselves understood and establish a new life for themselves. Language is the key to that new life, but linguistic fluency is rarely achieved without a cost. We teach classes where highly qualified doctors, accountants, physicists and teachers mingle with learners who are illiterate in their own languages and have never been to school. We must boost confidence and sooth injured feelings as learners settle into a new and challenging classroom environment. ESOL learners can vary in age from 16 to 70 and we must engage across the whole spectrum, keeping the teenagers motivated while spending time with an older learner who needs extra support.

We have to be experts in conflict resolution. Many learners are traumatised by war, unsettled by constant relocation and harried by the knowledge that they have left loved ones behind them. They can be a shifting, unsettled population, unsure of their status and liable to be moved on at a moment's notice. Learners often share stories with us that are far outside our own experience, and that shake us out of our own comfortable lives.

An ability to communicate verbally is essential but we also need to be skilled actors, adept at using gestures, mime and facial expressions to convey our meaning. Of course an excellent knowledge of English and how it works is vital, but there is more to teaching ESOL than grammar and vocabulary. We must help our learners to understand the world in which they find themselves, what constitutes acceptable social behaviour and how they fit in to a culture so very different from their own.

We have to be endlessly creative with limited resources, often delivering ESOL in community venues, sharing a space with the crèche, and competing for attention with a breast-feeding baby or a screaming toddler. There may be no interactive whiteboard, photocopier or DVD player, and a flip chart and board-marker are sometimes the only teaching tools available.

We need to appreciate that our western-oriented, student-centred teaching strategies may at first make very little sense to learners. Expectations of education vary, and many find the communicative language classroom a strange and threatening environment. Working in pairs or groups, acting out roles, playing games and watching video clips can be far removed from the rote-learning, teacher-led experience that many learners are familiar with.

Above all I think an outstanding ESOL teacher must possess a genuine passion for their subject and share an interest in the lives of all their learners, making everyone they teach feel valued and respected, regardless of background or ability.

Motivation

How teachers approach the issue of student motivation, be it intrinsic or extrinsic, is determined, in part, by the andragogical or pedagogical philosophical underpinnings of the educationalists' teaching and learning strategies. Barriers can arise when pedagogical methods and practices are applied completely or in part to situations that require andragogical dynamics.

Knowles (1984) points out that growing older, the mature adult becomes more independent, and wholly self-directing. 'When a person becomes older, his motivation to learn comes more from his own self' (p. 12).

Creativity and innovation: 14–19

All teaching needs to be creative and innovative and this is particularly vital when planning and implementing teaching and learning for the 14–19 age range. The model of outstanding teaching made by Ofsted relies on clear learning objectives which are explained and discussed at the start of the lesson, followed by activities that are appropriate for all students, engaging and well-paced and a plenary at the end of the lesson, designed to assess the quality of learning that has taken place. However, it is important to see the students not simply as children but as young adults and as such, planning for learning needs to draw on both pedagogical and andragogical strategies to engage and support young adults in the classroom. This move towards embedding creativity into the curriculum is often difficult, as college curricula often do not acknowledge the creativity and socially situated knowledge that learners bring into the classroom. As such, for many educationalists, the more traditional behaviourist and cognitivist theories of learning no longer fully resonate with the real purpose and value of education and our wider role in working most effectively with learners. Rather than the transmission of knowledge from expert to novice, to be recalled and reproduced, more contemporary theories of learning place the learner, not the instructor/teacher at the centre of the educational process, with the role of tutor to guide and support learners as they actively develop their ability to make meaning and construct deeper understanding.

Rather than communicating an objectivist view of knowledge, constructivist learning theories recognise the central role of the learner in constructing their own knowledge and dynamic understanding of the world through their own interactions and lived experiences. Education becomes a process of supporting learners to construct their own meaning based on their prior experiences, through interpretation, accommodation, assimilation and social-isation. Using multimodal approaches, which include poetry and images, can be a move towards reflection and transformation (Duckworth 2010). The use of multimodal literacies offers the expansion of the ways learners acquire information and under-stand concepts. Words, images, sound, colour, animation, video, and styles of print can be combined. Indeed as noted by Ingle and Duckworth (2013), quality teaching and learning can be enriched when focus is given to the development of a dynamic multimodal teaching and learning environment, which includes using a range of new communication technologies which have the potential to enhance the teaching and the learning experience for learners.

Respect

Fourteen- to nineteen-year-old students often show a developing demand for respect from their peers and the teachers they work with as they try to establish their own identity. Many students feel that teachers do not understand this desire (Blatchford 1996) and while the students increasingly see themselves as adults, their teachers may not always have the same view of them. It is important for the teacher to recognise the changing and individual needs of students and identify strategies which meet them.

Reflection and activity

Consider the strategies identified by Duckworth et al. (2012) and how you can create a jigsaw to meet the needs of your learners.

While students are in this transitional, adolescent phase there is a need to scaffold learning closely until the students have developed the skills to move their own learning forward. Breaking down activities and assignments into manageable 'chunks' will allow students to manage their learning, target-ing smaller goals which will then come together, in much the same way as you might complete a jigsaw. Beginning with corners, the underpinning essential knowledge and under-standing should be added, much like completing the outside of the jigsaw, matching up the straight edges. At this point, students may then be ready to begin work on the complete picture, using the support and expertise of their teacher to enable them to identify where each piece fits. Given the variety of students and abilities in most 14–19 classrooms, the level of scaffolding needed to support students will vary and much depends on the skill of the teacher to build effective relation-ships with their students, knowing when and how to support them and planning for individual needs and abilities in their classroom.

(Duckworth et al. 2012)

Andragogy and motivation

The assumptions of andragogy can lead to unrealistic and idealistic expectations about the behaviour of adults. According to Knowles (2005), adult students are more likely to be internally motivated, learning as a means of satisfying curiosity and for self-fulfilment, for example, rather than through external motivators such as quali-fications, career trajectory or financial rewards. If, as a teacher, your expectations are of highly motivated students, disengagement can be extremely challenging. The assumptions of andragogy have implications for the way in which adults are taught and the teach-ing methods used, which should be designed to make best use of student experiences and existing knowledge, such as discussion. Allowing adult students a voice is essential and provides a rich resource for the teacher which can be utilised. Harnessing such knowledge not only motivates adult students but also can have a profound impact on learner confidence.

Andragogical approaches to teaching can be liberating for both the students and teacher, according to Paulo Freire, a Brazilian educationalist (1921–1997). In Freire's challenge to the 'banking' system, he recommended a critical pedagogy model for teaching adult literacy (Freire 1993). Educationalist theorists have devel-oped this approach (see Giroux 1997; Lankshear and McClaren 1992; Lankshear 1993; Shor 1992, 1993). They have challenged prescriptive approaches to curriculum designs which do not take into account the history or background and needs of learners. These non-critical curriculums place emphasis on an instrumental approach ignoring the political, social, and economic factors that have conspired to marginalise the learners and the communities they live in. Duckworth (2013) argues that effective learning cannot be based on transmission from teacher to learner and must involve personal negotiation based on the learner's own goals and personal history.

Final thoughts ...

Many theorists believe the andragogy/pedagogy classification is not flawless, but they cannot agree on a viable alternative either. I would suggest that having an awareness of different approaches allows us to engage with learners in meaningful ways irrespective of their age. This interface between childhood and adulthood needs to be managed carefully to avoid the classroom becoming a 'battlefield' (Lumby and Foskett 2007). A meaningful way to address this is to view each individual and their needs as unique and tailoring a programme which may include aspects of what are considered andragogical and pedagogical models – a continuum of them both (and others) rather than the notion of one approach for adults and one for children and young people.

Further reading

Armitage, A., Bryant, R., Dunnill, R., Flanagan, K., Hayes, D., Hudson, A., Kent, J., Lawes, S. and Renwick, M. (2012) *Teaching and Training in Post Compulsory Education*. Maidenhead: Open University Press.
Freire, P. (1996) *Pedagogy of the Oppressed*. London: Penguin.
Hillier, Y. (2011) *Reflective Teaching in Further and Adult Education*. London: Continuum.

Websites

Institute for Learning: www.ifl.ac.uk
Department for Business, Innovation and Skills: www.bis.gov.uk
Alliance for Inclusive Education: www.allfie.org.uk

Chapter 3

Who are the learners?

Chapter objectives

This chapter provides an insight into understanding learners and their characteristics. In doing so it identifies diversity and access issues and discusses starting from where the learners are. It also explores approaches to learning and teaching.

Introduction

Further Education is diverse, rich and a fast changing landscape. Learners enter Further Education for many reasons. In the UK there has historically been a clear demarcation between the academic and vocational routes through education post-16. Generally vocational study is taken either on a part-time basis or full-time at Further Education colleges. Students who want to take academic qualifications such as A levels have the option to enrol in a school sixth form, a Sixth Form College or a general FE college. Clearly, a learner's choice of institution will be heavily determined by her choice of curricula given that the vast majority of students taking vocational qualifications post-16 enrol in FE colleges rather than schools (Stanton and Fletcher 2006).

Understanding learners and their characteristics

Knowing your learners is a vital part of being a great teacher and should not be underestimated as an afterthought or a bolt on. Knowing your learners and meeting their needs is bound in respecting their uniqueness and personal histories.

Learners' histories and biographies

Learners' histories and biographies can impact on their learning environments. As such teachers' awareness and sensitivity to the issues that learners bring into the classroom and the development of strategies for dealing with them effectively are important if the barriers are to be addressed (Barton et al. 2007: 137). Education has been shown to enhance confidence, contribute to personal development, promote health, social and political participation and lead to benefits in the public and private domains of learners' lives (Duckworth 2013). Tett et al. (2006: 81) reported that:

> *Learning and its benefits are dynamic in the sense that benefits gained in one domain such as education impact on functioning in other domains, such as family and community.*

Duckworth and Cochrane (2012) argue that the 'blame and the guilt' many learners feel when they 'fail' to achieve in the compulsory educational system 'is hardly surprising in today's neo-liberalist society, where myths of everyone having equal choice and options permeate through institutions and public life' (ibid.: 588). From my experience of living and working with learners from disadvantaged backgrounds, I believe that the notion of neo-liberalism and its implication that an individual is free to determine their own pathway, is limited by the impact of structural and historical inequalities: gender, race and class and other markers of identity that shape the learners' educational journeys (Leathwood 2006; Duckworth 2013).

For example, learners from socio-economically deprived areas may not have the same access to opportunities as those who live in more affluent areas who would be more able to attend high achieving state schools or receive a private education. Thus, school success may be seen as linked to 'the amount and type of cultural capital inherited from the family milieu rather than by measures of individual talent or achievement' (Reay et al. 2005: 19). For the children who face structural inequalities such as being poor, the choices they have on leaving school or college can be limited and can impact on their life chances, opportunities for future education or training and future employment. It is important for the teachers to be aware of the barriers to learning learners have faced and continue to face. For example, learners may carry negative labels from previous educational, working and personal experiences and bring with them 'fear of violence, threat and intimidation' (see Barton et al. 2007: 165; Duckworth 2013). Through effective support along their trajectory, in the private and public domains of their lives which include: home, the community, school, college and the workplace, they can build a better future. It is by returning to adult basic education, learners can turn their life around (McNamara 2007; Duckworth and Taylor 2013).

Importance of practitioners

The position of the teacher is not neutral; you can create an environment where learners' ideas and self-awareness flourish or diminish this. As Duckworth and Cochrane (2012) assert, 'Clearly, those who teach have the power to transmit their values, their world visions, their ideologies and prejudices; this makes the teaching-learning process a non-neutral one' (ibid.: 288). As teachers you can play a large role in undermining students' functioning, specifically through labelling. Labelling students can have an impact on learning and importantly on their confidence and self-esteem. Labelling theory, although initially applied to sociological studies of deviant behaviour by Howard Becker in the 1950s and 1960s, has been the subject of a great deal of research in the field of education in order to determine students' academic outcomes based on the labels they have been given in class and subsequently, the expectations that they have obtained by practitioners within their schools. Becker (1963) argues that it is not the individuals' actions but the social reaction to those actions that creates deviance. His ideas are important as they can highlight how those in a position of power (such as classroom teachers) can label individuals as deviant. This can lead to practitioners lowered expectations, as well as more negative stereotypes and attitudes toward the labelled.

The key to a supportive classroom environment is a teacher who is willing to challenge negative labels and in doing so establish a caring relationship with each student, learn about a student's individual needs and strengths, and offer the support and encouragement each student needs to reach their potential. Students with behavioural issues will benefit from teachers who are committed to an inclusive classroom, organised, plan for any potential challenges and establish a secure classroom where students feel valued. Part of feeling valued includes practitioners recognising and addressing the barriers to learning which students face and how this impacts on behaviour and motivation.

Starting from where the learners are

Inclusive teaching means recognising, accommodating and meeting the learning needs of *all* your students. This includes recognising that your students have a range of individual learning needs and are members of diverse communities; for example a student with a disabling medical condition may also have English as an additional language and be a single parent. Inclusive teaching avoids labelling and essentialising students into specific groups with predictable and fixed approaches to learning.

Reflection and activity

Consider how you address equality and diversity in the classroom.

Now read Claire Marsh's case study and identify the strategies she uses in her practice.

For the past two years, I have been working as a Psychology and Health and Social Care Tutor within the Access and Continuing Education Department, in one of the biggest Further Education colleges in the UK.

The Access department actively promotes social inclusion and believes it is crucial to support people, not just in their studying, but in their lives also. The Access department is often considered a 'second chance route' meaning that the student population is diverse. Students are aged 19+ and come from a variety of backgrounds.

'Equality and diversity' is a concept that has been driven over the past few years. I understand equality and diversity to be about actively preventing the exclusion of disadvantaged groups and ultimately empowering students to be independent lifelong learners. As a teacher in adult education I believe I contribute to this in many ways. The first thing to remember is that equality is not about treating everybody the same. It is about recognising and appreciating that everybody is different, and despite these differences, everyone should have access to the same opportunities. Essentially, it is part of our job as teachers to create a level playing field in order for all learners to achieve regardless of age, gender, race, disability, social class, nationality, the number of children they have and the things that have happened to them in the past.

I find that diversity in the classroom can be used to maximise the potential of each learner. I encourage learners to share their own experiences in order to promote inclusivity and celebrate diversity. Inclusivity is essential in creating a friendly and participatory learning environment. I like to include class discussions, group tasks and presentation activities in my lessons. This helps to facilitate cohesion, and I often place learners into groups to encourage communication with other class members. Learner diversity and experience is a precious learning tool and therefore it is important to build upon this as an educational resource. Luckily, psychology is a subject that lends itself to class discussions and debates where views and issues, such as stereotyping, can be countered.

For example, when covering a unit on communication in health and social care, I incorporated a session about cultural and language barriers within the local community. Also, another teacher and I organised a cultural awareness day where students brought in food and dressed up in traditional clothing in order to promote and celebrate diversity. These are examples of designing a curriculum that recognises and celebrates the cultural capital of learners (what they read, their culture, the music they listen to and so on) as well as promoting equality and diversity.

Another thing to consider in relation to equality and diversity is your teaching resources. Are they representative in terms of diversity? Do you use examples that are relevant to a range of cultures? Do the images/case studies/handouts you use include a range of people from diverse backgrounds? All these things, no matter how small, have an impact on how people see themselves and what they think they can achieve.

A classroom of adult learners can present a diverse range of ability, meaning that differentiation is a challenging, but useful and essential tool for effective teaching and learning. I include differentiated learning objectives in all lesson plans. The learning objectives are put in categories of 'all', 'most' and 'some' learners to allow for individual achievement. I believe it is important to share the learning objectives with learners; if done effectively, this works to empower learners and allow them to take ownership of their learning. In order for this to work, the learning objectives need to be phrased using a level of language that is accessible and that learners can engage with.

I also try to discuss subject terminology in a context that learners can relate to. This allows them to access, learn, and use, the meta-language of the subject. Learning subject terminology can be trickier for English as a second/additional/other language learners. I have a large proportion of EAL learners within all my classes. I often run extra language support sessions which are open to all students in order to discuss any key words/concepts covered in class. We often complete activities such as key words matching tasks or we spend time putting together posters or glossaries of key terms and their definitions.

I have taught learners who have hearing impairments, visual impairments, dyslexia, mental health issues and various other learning support needs. In each case I have worked closely with these learners to understand and provide individualised support specific to their learning needs. This usually involves liaising with student support services, for example, when arranging note takers and designing alternative handouts. Building good relationships with learners and other support staff involved is a key part of this process, especially when teaching adults. Learning should be based upon a consensus rather than instruction from the teacher; adult learners are often included in the decision making and teaching process and it is important that there is a good and supportive relationship between teacher and learner.

I often hear teachers complaining about embedding equality and diversity into their teaching practice and unfortunately it is sometimes perceived as more of a paper exercise and measure of institutional performance rather than any kind of social justice. But by embedding equality and diversity into our lessons we are mirroring what should be happening in wider society anyway, and when done effectively, it creates an enjoyable, happy and thriving learning environment.

Reflection and activity

Consider whether your teaching resources are representative in terms of diversity?

Do you use examples that are relevant to a range of cultures?

Do the images/case studies/hand-outs you use include a range of people from diverse backgrounds?

Embedding equality and diversity into your everyday practice is vital

Not only is it great practice it is also a requirement. The result of not implementing equality and diversity can result in damaging litigation and/or a Skills Funding Agency notice to improve as a result of an Ofsted inspection judgement of 'inadequate' for the overall effectiveness of the provision at the institution you are teaching. To be a brilliant teacher, 'equality and diversity' need to be a priority. They need to be integrated into your curriculum design: from session planning and teaching methods to assessment procedures; from inclusive resources and materials to teaching which focuses on discrimination, harassment and victimisation because of disability, race, gender, sexual orientation, transgender, religion or belief, age, culture etc. Your classroom should welcome diversity not isolate individuals.

Reflection and activity

Identify how and why you are/can be culturally responsive and motivational in your teaching.

You may have noted the following points:

- Create and sustain a safe, inclusive, and respectful teaching and learning environment.
- Respect diversity.
- Promote equitable and meaningful learning opportunities.
- Derive teaching practices from across disciplines and cultures.

Case study

Mike Bailey, a trainee teacher, shares his experiences of engaging learners through teaching History in a socially, culturally and historically responsive way.

The first point to consider when teaching History to learners in FE is their level of emotional maturity and their ability to appreciate the complexity surrounding sensitive topics. This is the reason why topics pertaining to World War I or the Holocaust are not generally taught on the National Curriculum until Key Stage 4 (The T.E.A.C.H. Report 2007). The rationale governing this choice to delay teaching such topics is that essentially the full extent of the depravity humanity has exhibited, particularly over the last century, is uncomfortable to acknowledge and the teaching of such modules must be done in earnest.

George Santayana's immortal words 'Those who cannot remember the past are condemned to repeat it' are often cited erroneously, yet his meaning is unquestionable; learning from our mistakes is a crucial skill we attribute to self-awareness and advancement. Yet without fully appreciating the past, both individually and as part of wider society, we cannot hope to learn from our more deplorable epochs any more than we can hope to be inspired by our greatest accomplishments. Learning lessons from the past can also provide us with a unique perspective on how to react to contemporary world issues. For example, the denunciation and criticism levied at Islam in the Western hemisphere since 9/11 is comparable to the persecution of Catholicism in England in the seventeenth century after the Gun Powder Plot. Therefore from studying the past, learners can truly appreciate that there are no unprecedented events occurring in the world today; there is always an historical precedent to compare them to because all human activity is driven by unchanging human nature. Therefore, it can be argued that the past may hold a great many answers to the pressing questions being asked today. And in terms of sociological advancement, before prevention must come prediction – if we can identify the reasons behind our less palatable annals of history then we can at least attempt to preclude similar events from occurring again. In short, it is worth remembering the epitaph

'Lest we forget' from the poem of Rudyard Kipling; learning from history involves digesting the good with the bad, and teaching History involves teaching learners to take collective responsibility for its entirety so that ultimately the messages we need to remember are passed from generation to generation *in memoriam* to the humanity that is so often overlooked in the pages of a textbook.

Teaching a module such as black Civil Rights in America often proves popular with learners and teachers alike; the enthusiasm learners have for this topic is correlative to the period being relatively recent, with key events in world importance happening within the last half century. According to one senior lecturer in History whom I have worked with and who has taught the topic for many years, the difficulty for today's learner lies in grasping that within our own lifetime, some people, in one of the most powerful nations in the world, a country that prided itself on being the world's defender of liberty, did not enjoy basic civil rights. From our twenty-first-century perspective we are unaccustomed to thinking back on a period where such bigotry and intolerance was rife in society, and not only this, was seemingly supported and endorsed by the law. Through the use of new and emerging technologies in the classroom, learners are able to view primary sources from the period, most notorious perhaps are the photographs printed concerning the murder of Emmet Till, a young boy who was kidnapped and brutally murdered while on a visit to the South, for simply conversing with a white shopkeeper. His mother's choice to display her son in an open casket took full advantage of the new media of television and photography, and the horrific photographs that featured in many news reports helped to formulate public support against such a heinous crime, and in doing so brought the Civil Rights movement much needed momentum. Similarly, today the same images are capable of having a profound effect, stirring emotion in the learner and helping to bring a human face to the events documented in the textbooks. As the Civil Rights movement is still relatively recent, many of the events transpiring within our lifetimes, there is a general consensus gained by teachers and learners that this history is still being written today; the full effects of racial discrimination in the USA in past decades are still influencing news coverage. In 1992, the beating of Rodney King led to the Los Angeles Race Riots, and in 2008 the United States elected its first black President in Barack Obama. Therefore the topic can best be described as a type of living-history, where we are teaching about a period that is still very relevant and issues that are still very prevalent in the world today. According to one learner I interviewed, studying the topic expelled her 'complacency' relating to her own civil liberties and allowed her to realise that a lot of the freedoms we take for granted had to be fought for and won during a bitter campaign amid oppression and social degradation, so it is fitting that Civil Rights is still taught almost in homage to the men and women, from Martin Luther King and Malcolm X, to the unnamed, unsung members of the Civil Rights move-ment in America, and through studying a panoramic assess-ment of social challenges to racism, legal challenges and political challenges, learners can begin to evaluate how success-ful society has been in eradicating racial discrimination in recent years.

Another module which strikes a chord with learners is the Suffragettes. Having had the opportunity to teach the topic to learners in Greater Manchester, it was interesting to see the impact that this had upon them, particularly the female members of the group. Like Civil Rights, there was a reaction of shock and repulsion from the learners who had difficulty accepting that the prejudicial attitudes of men towards women were so disproportionately executed in law and that less than one hundred years ago, women in our own country did not have the right to participatory democracy through the vote. Learning about the strife of women in this period, and the feats accomplished by the likes of Millicent Fawcett and Emmeline Pankhurst, enthuses female learners when they realise the lengths that women had to go to in order to achieve the same legal stature as men. And what truly reinforces the sense of injustice among learners is the realisation that even today, women are still barred from some professions in the armed forces etc. and receive less pay for doing the same work as men in others. This helps learners to realise just how relevant these topics are to today's society and hopefully inspires them to continue to support different campaigns for an end to social injustice.

Therefore with regard to subject matter it is clear that teaching modules in History relating to concepts of injustice, intolerance and prejudice can go a long way to help remedy these problems by informing learners of the historical struggles large groups of people have undertaken for equality, whether it be tackling prejudice based on race, gender, sexuality or religion, and how their struggles should inspire us to continue their campaign for tolerance and greater liberty. Another element of teaching History that is capable of motivating and inspiring learners is the teaching of local history. With relation to the Suffragettes, teaching such a module in Manchester, the birthplace of pioneers such as the Pankhurst family, allows learners to retrace the footsteps of these inspiring individuals and visit the places they did. It is a very human fascination we have with regard to tactile stimulation and being able to touch and feel the same things and walk among the same places that our historical heroes did. And although, as Marx maintained, 'the history of all hitherto society is the history of the class struggle', teaching local geographical history gives the learner a sense of more direct involvement with the topic, and the possibility that perhaps their ancestors were part of these campaigns for social justice and improvement.

When recognising the enormous lengths local people went to in order to campaign for greater equality it hopefully inspires and motivates learners to participate more in their local community as history can often be our common heritage. It is our ties to the past that bind us together in the present and they should continue to do so with the teaching of local history. Therefore, History as an academic subject has the potential to aid with community cohesion by reminding our learners of our shared inheritance from local groups in the industrial North, such as the Suffragettes and the Chartists. And with particular regard to offender learning, teaching social history to this group of people has the potential for enormous benefit; there is a therapeutic aspect to learning about the struggles of others that can aid with rehabilitation as history can increase awareness and enlightenment and put our own misdemeanours into perspective.

To conclude, teaching History provides us with an opportunity not only to inform our learners of the factual events that have occurred in times gone by, as this would be irrelevant without focusing on the issues surrounding them. Appealing to attitudes of social justice, liberty, the denunciation of prejudice and the struggle for social advancement which underpin all basic human endeavour gives these areas of history a relevance to all. Teaching about topics such as World War I and the Holocaust allows us to pass down important messages to each subsequent generation in the hope that we can prevent such horrors from occurring again and out of veneration to the ordinary men and women who made it their life's work, such as the Suffragettes and members of the Civil Rights movement, to improve the standard of living for all. When teaching and studying some modules of social history a key message emerges: all of us are born into a world that is divided in one way or another. Some of us have the strength to seek to heal those divisions – figures of adulation such as Martin Luther King and Emmeline Pankhurst. And while it is all too often a bitter and poignant reality that these figures do not live to see their visions accomplished, hopefully their stories inspire us enough to make sure that we continue their goal of a world united and free from intolerance. The British statesman Edmund Burke once said that 'All that is necessary for the triumph of evil is for good men to do nothing'. Hopefully, through the teaching of social history in the classroom, we can pass on the message that wherever we witness intolerance and prejudice it is the responsibility of us all to challenge this and to seek to eradicate it.

Reflection and activity

Consider how events and narratives from the past can promote equality, consciousness raising and motivation in the classroom.

Inclusive Teaching

Taking an inclusive approach when teaching will help to ensure that your teaching meets everyone's needs, enabling learners to learn effectively. As a result learners will feel that they belong in the classroom and the educational institution.

Relatively small adjustments to teaching practice can make a huge difference in terms of inclusivity. For instance ensuring notes and hand-outs for lessons are available in advance electronically; giving instructions verbally and visually and using a variety of learning activities in your teaching.

When considering inclusive approaches you may:

- take a comprehensive and coherent approach which is anticipatory and proactive
- have a strategy for delivering equal opportunities and diversity policies
- involve the whole organisation in your work
- match provision to student needs
- integrate regular reflection, review and refinement of strategies and methods that actively involve students with learning disabilities/difficulties
- recognise the learners' histories and build lessons that respond to and value them.

Reflection and activity

Consider why Inclusive Teaching matters.

You may have noted:

- Inclusive teaching is more likely to be BRILLIANT teaching.
- We live in a diverse society: education should reflect, promote and facilitate this in positive way which moves from deficit models.
- The Disability Discrimination Act (DDA) requires that institutions do not discriminate, and provide equality of opportunity for all students, including disabled students.

Reflection and activity

Read Mike Stoddart's case study and consider the strategies used to provide an inclusive teaching and learning environment. Are there additional strategies that you could use in your own specialism/context?

I have 23 years' experience in Post-Compulsory and Higher Education and have taught learners from pre-entry to post-graduate level. For most of my career I specialised in provision for students with learning disabilities and teacher education. I also have extensive managerial experience as a head of department and faculty director where I developed many successful partnerships with a range of public and private organisations. I am currently researching behaviour for learning and mentoring and coaching in FE.

In a nutshell: *A teacher in post-compulsory education; challenging but also stimulating and rewarding.*

Tony was a bright and determined student who wanted to complete a business studies course at a college in the north-west of England. He is registered blind and has no usable vision. The course team had no previous experience of teaching such learners and were understandably concerned regarding their ability to ensure Tony's success on the programme. The way forward was a collaborative approach that put into practice the principles of Inclusive Learning proposed as early as 1996 by Tomlinson. Meeting learners' individual needs is at the forefront of curriculum planning and delivery rather than expecting learners to fit into what has been traditionally offered:

> *By inclusive learning we mean the greatest degree of match or fit between how learners learn best, what they need and want to learn, and what is required from the sector, a college and teachers for successful learning to take place.*
>
> Tomlinson 1996

The response of the college was to facilitate professional development for the course team. This was devised and delivered well in advance of the start of the course by a partnership between the RNIB Education Department, the college Learning Support Co-ordinator and Tony himself. This equipped the team with some basic strategies for action but just as importantly, the confidence that they could rise to the challenge. Course materials were provided in advance and in Braille including the use of tactile charts and diagrams produced by the RNIB Transcription Services. A personal computer complete with specialist software enabled Tony to submit written work which could then be marked and returned for Tony to receive written assessment feedback via audio. Regular reviews were held to evaluate progress, identify issues and decide on further actions required. This was a model of practitioners engaging in action research to the benefit of the learner.

This collaborative and personalised approach together with Tony's talent and determination enabled him to succeed on the programme and progress to degree level. But the process had further positive results. In meeting Tony's needs the course team was able to more effectively meet the learning requirements of everyone on the course. They delivered the programme in imaginative ways that enhanced the learning experience for all. Success rates improved, the staff extended their repertoire of teaching skills and gained professional satisfaction in doing so. They also provided a model for other teams in the college to follow and highlighted the relevance of an inclusive approach for all learners.

Reflection and activity

Consider how you can use collaborative and personalised approaches in your practice.

Matching the teaching to the learning

The ways young people and adults learn have a great effect on their ability to acquire and apply knowledge, seek learning experiences, and enjoy participating in the education process. Learners have learning styles that best suit them. They also often have a preference for one style over another, but these preferences may vary depending on the situation and how learning objectives are to be achieved (see Chapter 5).

Principles of effective teaching and learning

The promotion of effective learning and teaching is a vital part of being a great teacher. Part of this process includes:

*   providing a supportive, meaningful and challenging environment;

- establishing worthwhile and productive learning partnerships;
- shaping and responding to a variety of social and cultural
  contexts.

As a teacher you will continually learn about the ways people
learn, the processes of learning and how individuals learn best.
You will learn about your learners as individuals, and learn with as
well as from your learners when pursuing knowledge together.
Effective learning and teaching is founded on an understanding of
the learner.

Understanding the learner involves

- identifying features of the learner's past and present experience
  and respecting the influence of these features on the learner's
  personal development;
- being strongly aware of factors such as location, gender, ethnicity, ability, disability, and socioeconomic and political
  circumstances – that place the learner within power relationships in the learning context as well as in society;
- recognising and supporting each learner's motivation and
  capacity to challenge and change her or his current
  circumstances;
- promoting continuity of experience by identifying, valuing,
  linking to, and extending from, prior knowledge and
  experience;
- taking into account relevance, meaning and application for the
  learner;
- identifying and meeting the needs, interests and abilities of
  individual learners and groups of learners;
- recognising and addressing the expectations and aspirations of
  the learner;
- recognising and promoting the creative potential of each
  learner;
- recognising an individual's preferred learning styles, and promoting the development of other learning styles;
- recognising and supporting the holistic development of the
  learner intellectually, emotionally, socially, physically, ethically
  and spiritually.

The Teaching and Learning Research Programme (TLRP) on Further Education (2012) highlighted ten principles of effective teaching and learning. These principles included:

1. Equip learners for life in its broadest sense. Learning should aim to help people to develop the intellectual, personal and social resources that will enable them to participate as active citizens and workers, and to flourish as individuals in a diverse and changing society. This implies a broad view of learning outcomes, and that equity and social justice are taken seriously.

2. Engage with valued forms of knowledge. Teaching and learning should connect with the big ideas, facts, processes, language and narratives of subjects so that learners understand what constitutes quality and standards in particular disciplines. This requires an understanding of learning that goes beyond the acquisition of skills.

3. Recognise the importance of prior experience and learning. Teaching should take account of what learners know already in order to plan their next steps. This means building on prior learning as well as taking account of the personal and cultural experiences of different groups.

4. Require the tutor to scaffold learning. Tutors should provide activities that support learners as they move forward, not just intellectually but also socially and emotionally, so that the learning is secure even after the supports are removed.

5. Need assessment to be congruent with learning. Assessment should help to advance learning as well as determine whether it has taken place. It should measure learning outcomes in a dependable way and also provide feedback for future learning, rather than being imbalanced by targets.

6. Promote the active engagement of the learner. A chief goal of teaching and learning should be the promotion of learners' independence and autonomy. This involves acquiring a repertoire of learning strategies and practices, developing a positive attitude towards learning, and gaining confidence in oneself as a learner. The work of FE tutors who support learners to do this should be recognised and rewarded.

7. Foster individual and social processes and outcomes. Learning is a social activity. Learners should be encouraged to work with others, to share ideas and to build knowledge together. Consulting learners and giving them a voice is an expectation and a right.

8. Recognise the significance of informal learning. Informal learning should be recognised as being at least as significant as
   formal learning and should be valued and used in formal
   education.
9. Depend on teacher learning. Tutors should themselves learn
   continuously to develop their knowledge and skill, and adapt
   and develop their roles, especially through classroom enquiry
   and other research. Teachers and tutors need more scope for
   professional judgement to decide 'what works', freedom to
   innovate, and room to take risks that encourage creativity in
   supporting learners' needs.
10. Demand consistent policy frameworks with support for teach-
    ing and learning as their primary focus – the tutor-learner rela-
    tionship should be at the centre of flexible, independently
    evaluated policies at national, local and institutional level. This
    involves creating a social partnership amongst all stakeholders
    and one which is less bureaucratic. They should be designed to
    make sure everyone has access to learning environments in
    which they can thrive.

(TLRP, 2008)

Reflection and activity

Consider how the principles inform your practice.

Your teaching strategies should include awareness of specific
learning difficulties (SpLD) which cover a wide variety of difficulties.
Many people use it synonymously with dyslexia (a difficulty with
words), but it is now generally accepted that dyslexia is only one of
a group of difficulties that may include:

- dysgraphia: writing difficulty
- dyspraxia: motor difficulties
- dyscalculia: a difficulty performing mathematical calculations
- attention deficit disorder, or attention deficit hyperactive disorder (ADD or ADHD): concentration difficulties with height-
  ened activity levels and impulsiveness
- Asperger's syndrome and autism: emotional behaviour or even
  social communication difficulties.

These learning difficulties typically affect a learner's motor skills, information processing and memory. However, note that no two individuals have the same combination of SpLD and it is impossible to generalise a description from one person to another.

Below Judy Hornigold, Dyscalculia Course Leader and Anne McLoughlin, Dyslexia Course Leader, both at Edge Hill University, share strategies for being a great teacher of learners with dyscalculia/mathematics difficulties and dyslexia/literacy difficulties.

Dyscalculia

The Department for Education (DfE) defines dyscalculia as: 'A condition that affects the ability to acquire arithmetical skills. Dyscalculic learners may have difficulty understanding simple number concepts, lack an intuitive grasp of numbers, and have problems learning number facts and procedures. Even if they produce a correct answer or use a correct method, they may do so mechanically and without confidence.'

Dyscalculia can be most simply described as dyslexia for numbers. It is thought to be caused by a difference in function of a specific area of the brain. People with dyscalculia have severe difficulty in dealing with the concept of number and are often unable to perform even the most basic arithmetic.

It is thought that between 3 per cent and 6 per cent of the population are dyscalculic, although many more have mathematical learning difficulties. People with dyscalculia may function perfectly well in all other areas, although it can co-occur with other difficulties in a similar way to dyslexia (BDA 2010).

Strategies to support people with dyscalculia

- Keep instructions short and simple.
- Highlight key numbers.
- Encourage learners to write down each stage of the calculation.
- Give extra time.
- Avoid overcrowded work sheets – use an aperture card to enable the learner to focus on one question at a time.
- Encourage problem solving and exploratory activites to develop mathematical understanding.

- Use manipulatives and concrete materials, don't move too quickly from the concrete to the abstract.
- Provide memory aids for times tables and key facts.
- Be aware of the learner's style of learning and adjust your teaching accordingly.
- Use multisensory teaching methods.
- Recognise and capitalise on strengths.
- Make sure that topics are revisited frequently.
- Foster an environment where mistakes are 'good' to reduce maths anxiety.

Dyslexia

About 10 per cent of the population have dyslexia, 4 per cent of those will be severely dyslexic (BDA 2012). The signs and symptoms of dyslexia are complex and these are often co-occurring with other learning difficulties. In classrooms learners with dyslexia may have difficulty carrying out instructions, have difficulty with reading or spelling, have a poor sense of rhyme and identifying sounds. They may be able to answer questions orally but have difficulty with writing the answer. Learners with dyslexia may also have difficulty processing complex language or instructions at speed. They may also have low confidence and self-esteem. However many learners with dyslexia can have areas of strength as well as weakness. Teachers have a duty to provide reasonable adjustments for anyone with a disability (Equality Act 2010). If these are put into place then many of the problems can be ameliorated and learners can reach their full potential.

Strategies to support people with dyslexia

- Use flexible groupings in classrooms.
- Initiate peer support.
- Use multisensory teaching methods.
- Use practical resources – coloured overlays, highlighters, word mats, ICT, clear fonts.
- Use visual checklists/timetables.
- Avoid copying from the board.
- Use alternative methods of recording.
- Give clear, repeated instructions.

- Allow extra time to complete tasks.
- Recognise strengths to promote self-esteem and confidence.

Final thoughts

When teachers strive to create inclusive college classrooms, they need to consider multiple factors, including course content, class preparation, their own classroom behaviour, and their knowledge of students' backgrounds and skills. Motivation is a key factor in stimulating students and providing an educational experience which offers them the opportunity to be productive and gives them self-respect. It can challenge the inequalities in the learners' lives and provide them with hope and aspiration which challenge the cycle of poverty and failure. As noted by Thomas et al. (2012), 'Students' backgrounds and experiences can have an impact on their learning. Teachers can use diversity positively to enhance the learning experience of individuals and the group, rather than seeking to normalise and elide difference' (p. 47). Being a brilliant teacher is about valuing diversity, your learners and the different knowledge, skills and practices they bring into the classroom.

Further reading

Collier, P. and Morgan, D. (2008) 'Is that paper really due today?': differences in first-generation and traditional college students' understandings of faculty expectations. *Higher Education* 55: 425–446.

Duckworth, V., Flannagan, K., McCormack, K. and Tummons, J. (2012) *Understanding Behaviour 14 +*. Maidenhead: McGraw-Hill Education.

Scales, P. (2012) *Teaching in the Lifelong Learning Sector,* Maidenhead: McGraw-Hill Education.

Stobart, G. (2005) Fairness in multicultural assessment systems. *Assessment in Education: Principles, Policy and Practice* 12(3): 275–287.

Websites

British Dyslexia Association: http://www.bdadyslexia.org.uk/

Equality and Human Rights Commission *How Fair is Britain?*:http://www.equalityhumanrights.com

Royal National Institute for the Blind: http://www.rnib.org.uk

Chapter 4

What to do on Monday morning/Wednesday evening/all day Friday?

Chapter objectives

This chapter offers an insight into planning and preparing for inspired learning. To support this it considers curriculum models and approaches to curriculum design. It also explores writing session plans and schemes of work to motivate your learners.

Introduction

The qualities that make up a brilliant teacher include passion, enthusiasm, resilience, and creativity. A great teacher is *empowered* and *empowering*.

Reflection and activity

Reflect on a time when you have been inspired by a teacher. List the qualities that made them a great teacher.

In my teaching career, making a commitment to offer students the best learning experience I can in the time we have together has been a key drive for me. Now as a teacher educator I often reflect on what makes a great teacher. I have watched many classes across subject areas, levels, abilities, ages and venues. The aspects of great teaching that have inspired me to write this book are described below.

What makes an inspiring and great teacher?

Passion

The passion for teaching can take two forms, a passion for supporting students to reach their potential and a passion for living from the perspective of your subject specialism.

Love the subject you're teaching

If you cannot bring yourself to arrive excited, enthusiastic and engaged for your lesson, how are you possibly going to get your students excited about it? But if you love it like it's the best job to have, because for you, it really is, your students will know. And, for the most part, they'll appreciate your enthusiasm.

Words of caution, though, don't think that all of your students are going to appreciate you all of the time, thank you and share your passion. It won't happen, and if you're teaching to get that external validation from your students, you're going to be disappointed. However, if you love your subject, and you take pleasure in teaching it well, you've got it in you to be a brilliant teacher.

Keep your ego in check

This is all about the learning process, don't take anything personally when the lesson doesn't run to plan, for example, you make a mistake or your student lets you know it by proving you wrong. Teaching is a very fulfilling and rewarding experience if you are mindful not to let your ego get involved.

Be engaging and relevant

Teaching is a two way street, if the student is not engaged, your efforts will have been wasted. You need to get a student interested, excited, and enthusiastic about learning. Get to know your students' desires, hopes, aspirations, dreams for now and the future and find out how you can teach in a way that is relevant to the things they want and the path they are taking. Know their journey and the steps they are taking or want to take.

Be clear and concise

Don't be 'woolly' and 'convoluted' by delivering unclear lessons and making a simple activity complicated. Lessons are not about how many big words you can use or how clever you sound; teachers can make things seem complicated to seem intelligent or superior. Don't do this; it is patronising and creates barriers. Remember this is not about you; make sure you make it as easy as possible for a student to learn and scaffold their knowledge.

Be organised

Be organised and be prepared for the lesson. Arriving without a plan and doing the lesson on the hoof is asking for chaos. Students will realise when you are not prepared and lose focus and respect. With a well-thought-out lesson plan and the focus, energy and enthusiasm of the teacher, the class will move along more smoothly and students will be more engaged.

When organising your lessons think about the sequence of the full programme (scheme of work). Start with the consideration of what you want to accomplish overall. Write out a plan for this. Once this has been carried out you can then plan by organising the schedule into months, weeks and days.

Be knowledgeable

If you are not knowledgeable on the content of the lesson you are delivering how can you teach it to someone else? Once you have your lesson objective, make sure you do the necessary research, so that you can be confident in your ability to teach. If you are teaching something that is highly specialised, make sure you make the effort to continue updating your knowledge and subject specialism. Subscribe to trade/subject specific magazines, read up on the latest developments, go to workshops, conferences, in-house staff development events, etc. Be pro-active not reactive.

Be inspiring

A teacher who can inspire their students has the potential to empower their students and open them up to possibilities they may never have considered, for example, progressing to university to study, a dream job or pursuing a hobby. Someone who is inspired will go to great lengths to see their objective carried out. Be inspired; be inspiring.

Be adaptable and resilient

Adaptability and resilience are important. The flow (and sometimes storm) of changes in educational policy over the last decade (see Chapter 2) and how they have shaped/shape the practices of teachers can be unsettling. Indeed change is the only constant; when circumstances change, learn to let go and embrace whatever is needed to progress. Do this in an empowered way and keep abreast of change; for example, keep ahead in your own personal and professional development. You may consider carrying out practitioner research to build up an evidence base that shapes your lessons and allows you to be an active player in change whilst also generating your own knowledge (for an example of practitioner research in the LLS, see Tummons and Duckworth 2012).

Maintain good humour

Bring yourself to class every day with the right mindset. Coming to class angry and with resentment, for whatever reason, will hinder your progression and that of your students. As teachers we must be able to put such things aside during class time. Though there will be times when you will want to scream, remember that this should not be a part of your lesson, even if the source of your anger is a student's action. Always be calm and act with integrity.

Turn up to your lesson with your sense of humour and be yourself. Humour draws students in, motivates, raises the dynamics in your class. Using humour can be a good way to give students respite from challenging subject matter.

Remember be authentic – be yourself!

Quality and teaching

In this Ofsted era many of us don't remember a period when schools and colleges were not regularly judged, assessed and graded. Today this is a central part of the business of school leadership and management. Teachers arrive into the workplace prepared to be scrutinised by peers, management, inspectors and their own students.

The observation of teaching and learning is a fairly new phenomenon in Further Education (FE) in England. It is only over the last two decades that FE colleges have witnessed its extensive use. Yet in this short space of time it has become the foundation of colleges' quality assurance (QA) and quality improvement (QI) systems for teaching and learning. One of the key drivers of this reform agenda has been the prioritisation of teaching and learning as the basis on which to build ongoing improvement across the sector (Bathmaker and Avis 2005; Colley et al. 2007; Finlay et al. 2007). The writing of lesson plans and schemes of work is an integral part of a teacher's role and can be viewed as a means to monitor quality of teaching and learning. However, the part they play can be contentious. In a low trust environment there is a tendency for observation of teaching and learning, which includes paperwork, to be aligned with the notion of 'hierarchical surveillance' (Foucault 1977) (for example, in the context of inspection and Quality and Assurance schemes). However, on the other hand they can be regarded as very positive and valued in high trust environments and offer really valuable learning tools for encouraging reflective practice and critical professional dialogues between peers (Hammersley-Fletcher and Orsmond 2004, 2005; Wragg 1999). In my experience, having open and professional dialogues (which includes sharing practitioner research) with your colleagues can be most valuable and worthwhile. Sharing best practice, personal experiences and research on topics which include shaping the curriculum, lesson plans and resources is part of this on-going dialogue. So, when Ofsted comes knocking on your classroom door, you are ready and empowered. Not because you have been coerced, but because you are in a community of practitioners who want to be great teachers and be fully prepared to cater for the diverse and changing needs of your learners in order for them to succeed in their goals.

Reflection and activity

Swap a lesson plan, resource and scheme of work with a peer. With a focus on sharing best practice, discuss your different approaches to lesson planning and resource development.

In the next section we will explore some of the practicalities together and consider curriculum issues and lesson planning in more detail. It may be helpful if you have a lesson plan and scheme of work at hand as we reflect on and discuss the points.

Curriculum issues: Definitions and boundaries

Curriculum is a complex and contested concept. It derives from the Latin word for a track or course (hence 'course of study') and it has tended to be used to refer to some specified route or pathway through an area, especially a piece of learning. At its simplest, it is often used to mean the same as a programme of study or a scheme of work. Yet in recent years it has taken on other meanings.

Some models of the curriculum are like flow diagrams for course planning.

The following may be familiar to you:

A systems model of course design

Programme Aims and Objectives

↓

Assessment

↓

Student Needs

↓

Methods and Resources

↓

Evaluation

Curriculum models and course design

This idea of a curriculum model acts as a systematic guide to course design. There may be disputes about the number of boxes, their order, or whether the process would be better expressed as a circle with evaluation feeding back into the next stage of programme planning. It is essentially about the planning *process* related to programmes or courses.

Other approaches to curriculum use the word to cover much more.

Curriculum may be used to refer to the whole complex of processes and forces which might constitute the role or the offer of an FE college. This *inclusive* definition is valuable for making links between different things, for example, marketing and student support, but it could amount to saying that curriculum is whatever schools or colleges actually do.

Reflection and activity

How would you define curriculum?
  List the factors which contribute to your subject specific curriculum.

Curriculum and pedagogy

One traditional way of limiting the idea of curriculum is to distinguish between curriculum and pedagogy. Here pedagogy is used to refer to the way things are taught, i.e. choice of methods, resources, relations with students, while curriculum is reserved for the *content* of the learning. This distinction is clear when we think of traditional exam boards like the EDEXEL or City and Guilds. Generally they saw their job as laying down what was to be taught (curriculum), e.g. which aspects of geography or which plumbing skills. They avoided saying very much about how it was to be delivered to the student (pedagogy).

Similarly, at least in its early days, the government-prescribed National Curriculum was made up of lists of content, e.g. the Battle of Hastings must be taught in History, Shakespeare must be taught in English. They did not specify pedagogy – this was left to teachers' professional judgement.

In recent years especially in post-16 education this distinction has broken down, because in many cases it is hard to distinguish what is taught from how it is taught. Take for example group or team work skills. The requirement that these must be part of every student's experience in college or university means that there is a need to deal with curriculum *content* – students need to learn *about* groups, as well as *method* – they need to learn *in* groups.

Reflection and activity

Identify elements of your teaching which are both content and process as described above.

Curriculum as planned learning

This gives us then the possibility of a definition of curriculum which lies between the all-embracing notions and the narrower idea of course content. Curriculum is *planned learning* – i.e. it is all those aspects of a student's experience which are intentionally designed to bring about learning.

This stress on intention allows us to exclude all the *accidental* aspects of the student's experience. They learn the fastest way to travel to college; they learn that gravy left on the refectory counter too long tastes vile, that however much they spend on new trainers there will always be someone who has a better pair.

It still includes the fact that we intend students to learn how to work in groups, how to organise their time, how to read effectively for meaning, etc.

Hidden curriculum

This leads on to a further issue in defining curriculum – the concept of *hidden curriculum*. Writers on education, particularly sociologists, have stressed that much of what we learn at schools and colleges is unintentional from the teachers' point of view but still has a powerful impact on students and plays a major part in their preparation for adult life. This is called the hidden curriculum and it consists of all those structures, procedures, routines, and regulations which are never written into course booklets but which convey powerful messages to students. For example, what does it tell students about our equal opportunities policy if all the senior posts in the college are actually held by white males? What do pin ups on the staff room wall, or the lack of a female toilet say to female students entering a college department in an area of traditionally male employment? If students with learning difficulties are encouraged to use the college refectory at different times from the rest of the college what message is conveyed about 'inclusive learning'?

Learning boredom

Read what Jack Common had to say about his elementary education in Northumberland at the turn of the century.

I had acquired the one faculty with which every school infallibly endows its pupils, that of being bored. It is very important, of course that every child should in the course of time become fitted up with this negative capability. If they didn't have it they would never put up with the jobs they are going to get, most of them, on leaving school. Boredom, or the ability to endure it is the hub on which the whole universe of work turns . . .

We learn reading and boredom, writing and boredom, arithmetic and boredom, and so on according to the curriculum, till in the end it is quite certain you can put us in the most boring job there is and we will endure it.

Jack Common, *Kiddar's Luck,* Turnstile Press 1951,
quoted in D. Hargreaves, *The Challenge for the
Comprehensive School:
Culture Curriculum and Community,* RKP 1982

Reflection and activity

What does Jack Common's account say about the relationship between the real curriculum and the hidden curriculum?

What might be the value to society as a whole of such a curriculum?

Understanding the hidden curriculum

Many writers have emphasised the power and importance of the hidden curriculum, which some see as transmitting the values of an oppressive capitalist society (e.g. Bowles and Gintis 1976) or producing adults who blindly accept authority and their dependence on experts (Illich 1973). Authority structures in the school, the competitive nature of much learning, the 'learning as a commodity' approach to assessment and exams are all seen as producing undesirable effects which sometimes contradict the official version of the aims of education (independence, self-reliance, community spirit, etc.).

Reflection and activity

Can you identify any such negative characteristics of the hidden curriculum in your own area of teaching?

How does this negative aspect of the hidden curriculum affect strategies to promote inclusion?

Is there sometimes a 'hidden curriculum' contradiction between what we say about students thinking for themselves and what we reward, e.g. in assessment?

However the hidden curriculum need not be seen only as a negative aspect of educational institutions.

The hidden curriculum and values

The principal of an American High School hands this letter to new teachers when they start at his school:

Dear Teacher,

I am a survivor of a concentration camp. My eyes saw what no man should witness:

Gas Chambers built by learned engineers. Children poisoned by educated physicians. Infants killed by trained nurses. Women and babies shot and burned by high school and college graduates.

So I am suspicious of education.

My request is:

Help your students become human. Your efforts must never produce learned monsters, skilled psychopaths, educated Eichmanns. Reading, writing, arithmetic are important only if they serve to make our children more human.

(quoted in Richard Pring, *Personal and Social Education in the Curriculum*, 1984)

Reflection and activity

> How far can the hidden curriculum carry positive messages which go beyond the official course content?

Models of curriculum – what is a model?

When we want to examine any aspect of behaviour or any complex system it is often useful to use a *model*. This can be a real thing, e.g. for architects or shipbuilders it is useful to actually make a version of the planned building or vessel. In other cases the model is symbolic, that is, it replicates the processes and procedures on paper, or increasingly these days via software. This idea of a model as an *imitation of the real thing* useful for planning and criticism, can be extended to refer to a *generalised version of a type*, which indicates the broad characteristics and categories of a range of examples. For example we might talk about the model of a car being a Ford Mondeo, because all Mondeos have certain characteristics in common, even though each actual car may be unique.

This last is the sense in which people talk about a *curriculum model* – it is a kind of template which tells us something about a range of courses planned according to the model without altering the fact that each programme is totally individual.

The model (e.g. *a modular curriculum*) tells us some of the information we need when looking at a programme and provides a guide for planners. If you wish to write a programme according to a particular model (e.g. a competence based curriculum) then there are certain guidelines which need to be followed, certain principles which will govern the choices you make. These don't mean that all competence based programmes are identical – simply that they have characteristics in common.

These guidelines and principles are useful to the *planner* but they are also vital to the *evaluator*. Unless you know what kind of programme a particular course was trying to be it is difficult to know whether it achieved its aims.

Product and process

One debate in curriculum planning which can be seen as a clash of models is the apparent conflict between *process* and *product*. Most of you will be familiar with *product* based curriculum models. These stress that what matters in curriculum is what the learning produces, i.e. the outcome of the programme. In the 1950s and 1960s particularly in the US this view was strongly associated with the behavioural theory of learning (e.g. Skinner 1953) and the idea of tightly specified learning objectives. Generally, introductory teaching programmes lay a great stress on the ability to write sound objectives as a professional discipline so it is likely you have encountered this approach before. In more recent years this product approach has been most commonly found in curriculum models which stress the importance of learning outcomes or competences.

Process and product – A debate about models

Product

Pro

The key feature of a product model is that its primary concern is with the measurement of *outcomes* – what is different about the learner at the end of the process. Hence the stress on pre- and post-programme assessment and measurability.

Product models offer a systematic, clearly structured, accountable curriculum model. They allow curriculum planners to show students and other outsiders what *difference* the programme will make.

Anti

On the other hand critics of this approach have argued that this presents an 'impoverished' view of the richness and unpredictability of learning. Learning is a voyage of discovery involving the whole human being. It cannot be circumscribed by the narrow criteria of outcomes and objectives (Stenhouse 1971, 1975).

As Stenhouse argues, specifying objectives for arts and cultural subjects ignores the whole point of what is involved in responding to a work of art, such as, Hamlet, a Picasso painting or piece of modern dance. This pre-specification may seem more practicable in science or technical subjects but even here critics would say it tends to promote *'right-answerism'* rather than critical individual thinking.

Process

Pro

Process models allow planners to talk about what actually happens – the experience of being on the programme. They allow for people to change and for people to learn things that the tutor never anticipated.

They encourage creativity and 'thinking for yourself'. They allow students at different levels of ability to learn together, each taking what they want from the experience. They develop transferable thinking, problem solving and teamwork skills.

Overall they are true to what really happens in an educational process.

Anti

Process models are inherently unaccountable. Students want to know what they will be able to do at the end of the course not what fulfilling and enriching experiences they will have while they are on it.

Employers and 'purseholders' want to know what they are paying for. Many process aims are unmeasurable and thus subjective and not assessable in a fair, reliable way. If a student can *do* something why should we be concerned about how they got to be able to do it?

Process models are just an excuse for self-indulgent teachers who do not want to measure their outcomes.

Organising knowledge: subjects, integration, modularity

A major question for all curriculum models is structure and differentiation.

How do we 'divide' up the curriculum into separate elements or aspects in order to teach it? What principles underlie this dividing process? There are different approaches:

1.   the basis of the knowledge

    • cognitive-affective-psychomotor (Bloom's taxonomy)
    • evidence-based (what rules of evidence?)

- convention-based (e.g. accountancy rules)
- opinion-based (different perspectives or value systems)

2. the 'difficulty' of the knowledge

- levels, e.g. in modular credit schemes
- grades, e.g. degree classification
- ideas of progression and cumulative development

Levels of knowledge – questions to consider

(Why) are quadratic equations 'harder' than long division?
(Why) is geology 'harder' than art?
(Why) is working out the return on a five horse accumulator bet (minus tax) easier than trigonometry?

Three Common Approaches to differentiating the curriculum

A. Subject-based

This is a traditional view of knowledge as 'naturally' divided into different subjects which are 'realms of thought' (cf. what the philosopher Paul Hirst (1974, 1993) calls *forms of understanding* or what Phenix (1964) calls *realms of meaning*) clearly different from each other, requiring different approaches, skills, attitudes etc. This approach is familiar because it is reflected in traditional school timetables, university departments and to some extent in arguments about the National Curriculum and in recent proposals in HE for subject 'benchmarking'.

What is there about engineering which makes all courses called engineering similar? According to this view the key unit of differentiation is the subject. Subjects have their own 'inner logic' and it is the job of the teacher to induct people into that 'way of thinking about the world'.

Advantages

1. Subjects provide identity and common understanding. 'We're all geographers here!'
2. They provide clear routes of progression for knowledge. Go from GCSE Art to A level Art to an Art Foundation to an Art degree, etc.

Disadvantages

1. Real life is not divided up into 'subjects'. Real problems 'merge' different subject concerns.
2. *Vocational* learning is inevitably cross-subject – this leads to 'hybrid' disciplines like medicine, engineering, journalism.
3. Subject loyalties may detract from meeting student needs.

B. Integration

The idea of an integrated curriculum suggests that curriculum should start out from real situations and problems and involve 'subjects' only in so far as they are relevant to the core topic. The classic example of this approach is 'progressive' primary school teaching based on TOPICS, where the Maths, English, Science, Social Skills, Art and Design are taught *through* a theme or topic like dinosaurs.

Advantages

1. Real life is integrated; learning can be based on real issues, problems, jobs.
2. Barriers can be broken down between specialisms and different perspectives can be brought to bear on particular cases, e.g. the Open University programme, 'Culture and Industrialisation' looks at 19th-century Britain from the point of view of Art, Literature, Economic and Social History, Engineering and Design, Architecture, Agriculture etc.
3. Subjects cross-fertilise each other. People in one subject area can learn from contact with the perceptions of another subject, e.g. designers and engineers discussing the building of a bridge or psychologists and physiologists looking at the effects of tiredness on athletes.
4. All subjects merge into other subjects at their highest level, e.g. biology into chemistry; chemistry into physics; physics into mathematics; mathematics into philosophy.

Disadvantages

1. There are no clear boundaries, limits, routes. This can confuse. 'You can't see the joins.' Students can become confused about which set of criteria they are applying in any given case.

2. There is not such a strong basis for common identity and belonging. ('I am an integrated vocational skills teacher.')
3. 'Subject loyalists' feel their subject is not given due credit, not properly developed, somehow emptied of its real value.
4. Problems of access: dropping in and out, continuity and progression.

C. Modularity

Here the curriculum is divided into 'blocks' of study, each of which has a given value. These blocks can be collected like stamps or a hand of cards to assemble a whole course or qualification. Examples include CATS (Credit Accumulation and Transfer) schemes in HE and of course A/AS Levels since Curriculum 2000.

Advantages

1. More efficient use of resources.
2. Better access through 'drop in' and 'drop out'.
3. Better 'fit' to student needs – 'empowers learners'.
4. Integrates full- and part-time learners.
5. Allows for more curriculum innovation.

Disadvantages

1. 'You don't get to the *core* of the subject discipline.' Key aspects (e.g. Key Skills or generic learning) may 'fall between the cracks'.
2. It is hard to make connections if you don't know where your students come from or are going to.
3. Varied student backgrounds produce *difficult* groups.
4. Need for high level of curriculum guidance and perhaps counselling.
5. Loss of a sense of 'belonging' – provided by common subjects or common experiences.

Competence

The Competence Based Education and Training (CBET) movement emerged out of US approaches to vocational training and began to spread into the UK in the 1970s and 1980s. It was strongly boosted by the commitment of the MSC in the 1980s to restructure apprenticeships in a way which ended time-serving and introduced 'tests of competence' (Manpower Services Commission 1981), and then by the founding of the National Council for Vocational Qualifications and the introduction of the GNVQ.

Competence models

Competence models of the curriculum are based on real jobs or roles. Work roles are described in terms of what the worker needs to be able to do ('perform, not just know about or understand'). These roles are judged in terms of the standards *actually expected* in employment and should ideally be assessed in *real working environments*. The key to developing a competence-based programme then is *role analysis*. It is necessary to break a role down into all its necessary elements. This is carried out under the NVQ framework by *lead bodies* who break up a work role for a particular area into key *'units'* and constituent *'elements'* of competence are constructed.

Each element should be accompanied by a set of *'performance criteria'* which 'identify only the essential aspects of performance necessary for competence' and range statements which 'express the various circumstances in which the competence must be applied and may detail for example differences in physical location, employment contexts or equipment used' (NCVQ 1991).

Problems of competence models (based on Saunders 1995)

1. Relevance

There is a tension in the idea of a national qualification structure which is based on job specific competence. The more specific a competence is (i.e. the more it is tied to a particular job in a particular firm on a particular site, the more valued it will be by employers – the more relevant it will be seen as being ('learning how things are done round here'). However the more *specific* it is the more problems it raises for a *national* qualification system. Can it be transferable?

2. Role of 'knowledge'

'Role performance dominates and is seen as a composite of skills knowledge and understanding. Knowledge and understanding underpin performance and where possible are to be tested through it" (Hodkinson 1992: 31).

Competence based approaches 'tend to reduce job competence to atomised observable *behaviours*' (Norris 1991). These miss the true nature of work roles.

It isolates or dismembers job-related action and discourages seeing the job as a whole integrated task (a holistic view). It diminishes the status of knowledge and understanding (broadbased education) which serves as a basis for flexibility and further learning.

3. Verification

If work tasks are complex and involve subtle ethical and interpersonal decisions, it is difficult to see how a competence-based assessment can do them justice. This criticism is made by Winter (1993) in his discussion of social workers, but could be generalised to all professional work using the model advocated by Schön who puts forward the idea of the 'Reflective Practitioner' (Schön 1983).

4. Control

Competence models miss the fact that actual work is not a simple mechanical process. Work takes place in a complicated web of social relationships and understandings, an informal culture which cannot be reduced to statements of measurable outcome. Jones and Moore (1993: 392) claim that competence leads to skills being 'disembedded from everyday social relationships and cultural practices'. They see this as part of a managerial strategy to exert more control over the work process.

5. Occupational effectiveness

Saunders (2006) argues, 'The problem for the proponents of the competence approach is that it actually cannot deliver what it promises. Observable job performance can never yield the collection of abilities which constitute "being good at your job"'. Competences compare with real jobs in the way that a robot may imitate a real person but not quite capture the essence.

Saunders' study of competence-based schemes found that while many people thought that being involved in qualifications-based programmes enhanced their self-esteem, '. . . A direct improvement in work effectiveness was not a perceived outcome' (Saunders 2006, citing Otter 1994).

6. Learning Process

Competence ignores *process* so has little to say about how people get to be competent. Technically the competence movement is about *accrediting* skills not *improving* them. '*You can't fatten a pig by weighing it.*'

If learners are directed to learn new skills that will be monitored and assessed, then the assessment misses the vital opportunity to reflect the reality of current work practices and subsequently will not qualify existing competence (Saunders et al. 1990, Saunders 2000, Saunders 2006). Giving people certificates for what they already do may well improve morale but it does not of itself raise skill levels. The danger may be that in ever more closely defining the methods for assessing skills we lose sight of the need to *improve* them.

Do I really need a scheme of work?

Unfortunately the 'Scheme of Work' has been devalued by its bureaucratisation and the belief of many teachers that it exists only to satisfy managers and Ofsted inspectors. However, I would argue that it is an essential part of the teacher's tool box. It is the teacher's equivalent of the builder's plan and the architect's drawings. It is a working document. It is not absolute, just as building plans can be changed up to a point. It is made to be messed with, to be annotated and scrawled all over. It is the most useful evaluation tool you can have, because given that most of us repeat courses year on year, reference to last year's well-worn Scheme is an excellent guide to how to change things for this year.

Reflection and activity

Lindsey Marsh, a teacher trainer, shares her tips and what should be included in a scheme of work.

Analyse how the existing scheme meets curriculum requirements.

Meeting curriculum requirements: This could be through specific reference to Unit/Module numbers and/or specific learning outcomes and assessment strategies/timings. You might comment on/identify the effectiveness of 'flow' of the existing scheme – has sufficient time been allowed for specific topics? Does the scheme allow for increasing difficulty (moving from lower to higher levels of knowledge and understanding)? Do topics follow each other in a logical fashion?

Meeting the needs of learners: This could be through the Teaching and Learning (T&L) strategies used. Is there a variety of T&L activities that incorporates different learning styles? How are different learner levels supported? Are specific learning support activities/strategies identified? Is there identification/explanation of how Every Child (Learner) Matters (EC(L)M) elements are supported? Is there incorporation of new and emerging technologies? Are opportunities for formative/summative feedback identified?

How are equality and diversity supported? Is there an induction period at the start of the course? How are Equality and Diversity (E&D) issues highlighted to learners? Are ground rules negotiated/made clear? Are learners given information about how they can get extra support if required? Are individual tutorials incorporated into the scheme? Do the identified resources support E&D (do they challenge stereotypes in gender for example)? Are group tutorials incorporated into the scheme? If so, do they address E&D and/or EC(L)M issues?

Reflection and activity

The above are examples only; it is not an exhaustive list. Can you think of any more information which you may wish to include in a scheme of work?

Now look at former trainee teacher Samantha Catterall's Scheme of Work (appendix 1). You might want to use this pro-forma to develop your own great scheme of work.

Case study: Vicky Duckworth

Below I draw on my experience of teaching adult literacy in a college in the north-west of England and developing a critical curriculum.

Having been born, brought up and living in the emotional and geographical landscape of the learners, I am immersed in their communities. This immersion allowed me, as a practitioner, a critical positioning whereby I have insider knowledge of their lives, motivations, pressures, hopes and dreams (see Giroux 1997; Macedo 1994; Shor 1992). It is from this position the critical model moves towards the learner being the co-producer of knowledge. In doing so it shifts away from teacher-directed, top-down, commonly imposed and standardised assessments that prescribe the same for all students, regardless of their ability, values, ethnicity, history, their community requirements or their specific contexts. Instead it takes an egalitarian approach, whereby there is a sharing of power between the teacher and the student in learning, the curriculum, its contents and methods. Freire (1993) proposed to do this via 'culture circles'. A 'culture group' is a discussion group in which educators and learners use codifications to engage in dialectic engagement for consciousness raising, liberation, empowerment and transformation. Education for liberation provides a forum open to the empowerment of learners, teachers, and the community, while also providing opportunities for the development of those skills and competencies without which empowerment would be impossible.

Reflection and activity

Consider strategies for facilitating learners to help shape the curriculum, its contents and methods.

What about planning for my lessons?

A lesson plan is a structure for a lesson. Imagine that the lesson is journey, and the lesson plan the map. It shows the paths you will travel: where you start, your middle, your finish. Lesson plans can be the thoughts of the teachers (and when done in a democratic way driven by the thoughts of their learners). They state what they hope to achieve and how they will achieve it. Lesson plans can take many shapes, from very structured (often novice teachers) to key notes (often very experienced teachers). Whatever the degree of experience it is important that all teachers take the time to think through their lessons before entering the classroom.

The reasons why planning is important include:

- Planning facilitates you to tailor your teaching strategies and materials to meet the needs of your class.
- Planning enables you to predict possible problems that may occur in class and how to deal with them.
- Planning is a way to gain the respect of your students. If you are prepared your students know; if you are not prepared they also know.
- Planning is a part of being a professional. Your students will expect you to be professional, much the same way you expect them to be motivated and learn.

Without planning the lesson could turn into chaos without learners having any clear idea of what they are doing or indeed why. A key aspect to planning is that you know your aims and objectives of the lesson and how the lesson's journey will meet them. You need to have a clear idea on what you want to achieve for your class and importantly what you want your students to do at the end of the lesson which they couldn't do before.

Reflection and activity

Consider the questions you ask about your lessons.
List the key features included in your lesson plan.

You may have asked:

- Have I set meaningful objectives?
- Have I included a range of teaching and learning strategies to inspire and motivate your learners?

- Have I used a range of assessment strategies?
- Have I personalised the curriculum to take into account the individual need/levels?
- Do I have a motivational plenary?
- Have I developed and maintained a challenging and inspiring pace which used every minute to facilitate learners engagement and progress

Reflection and activity

Consider the questions you ask about your objectives.
List the key features of your objectives.

You may have asked:

- Are my objectives the correct description of what's happening in the class and justification of why it is being done?
- Do they fit with my Scheme of Work framework? Have I considered the flow and content of the delivery in terms of what was delivered in the previous lesson and what will be delivered in the next?
- Have I identified how each of the activities in my session will facilitate my learners' progress to achieving the objectives?
- Do my objectives enable all learners to reach their full potential by proving differentiation and stretch?
- Are my objectives meaningful and importantly realistic?

Reflection and activity

Consider whether you include a range of strategies in your learning plan.
List the range of strategies you may use in your lesson plan.

You may have included:

- teacher-led listening
- peer-led input

- peer discussion (in pairs/groups) and kinaesthetic sharing of information
- teacher assessment by questioning strategies, for example, open and scaffolded questioning, independent writing, peer assessment
- use of technology, for example the showing of YouTube clips, Petcha Kutchi presentations, etc.
- summative assessment through group quiz.

Reflection and activity

Consider whether you have promoted ways of collaborative learning whereby learners can share information.
List strategies for promoting collaborative learning.

You may have included:

- the group sharing ideas with each other
- sharing your experiences with the class
- group enquiry to get information from textbooks and the internet.

Reflection and activity

Consider whether you have implemented a range of assessment strategies.
List a range of assessment strategies.

You may have included:

- teacher/group/peer sharing of assessment criteria
- formative/summative
- peer feedback to each other – for example, the strengths of the lesson, what could be improved
- feedback on what the group have learnt/what they would like to re-visit at the next lesson
- How could you make the lesson even better?

Reflection and activity

Consider whether you have personalised your lesson plan.
Identify strategies for personalising a lesson plan.

You may have included:

- know your class
- scaffolded objectives, time allowed, the number
- positioning of the group: seating arrangements/grouping/pairing (more able/less able/mixed ability groupings)
- differentiating questioning strategies to promote inclusion of all, stretching and challenging
- extension tasks to stretch each learner to reach their potential.

Reflection and activity

Now look at Samantha's lesson plan (appendix 2) and identify features that you may find useful in your lesson planning.

Final thoughts

What is it that inspirational teachers do differently? In short, they plan for their learners to be inspirational. Many teachers speak with enthusiasm about stimulating and influential teachers who inspired their lives and now they want to do the same. Students clearly understand the importance of teachers being kind and open, and cultivating positive relationships with students. As an adult literacy teacher and teacher educator, I have found that my students enjoy hearing and sharing experiences. As members of society it is important that we share and learn from each other all of the way through life. This should never stop in an educational setting.

Further Reading

Coffield, F. (2009) *All you ever wanted to know about teaching and learning but were too cool to ask*, UK: LSN.

Eastwood, L., Coates, J., Dixon, L. and Harvey, J. (2009) *A Toolkit for Creative Teaching in Post-Compulsory Education*, London: Open University Press.

Marsh, C.J. (2009) *Perspectives: Key concepts for understanding curriculum*. London: Falmer Press.

Websites

TES Resource Bank: www.tes.co.uk/resources

Infed: Curriculum Theory and Practice: http://www.infed.org/biblio/b-curric.htm

The manifesto 'Every Woman's Right to Learn' (NIACE): http://www.niace.org.uk/womenlearningmanifesto

Learning and violence: http://www.learningandviolence.net/

Chapter 5

What will actually happen?

The objectives of this chapter

This chapter provides an insight into approaches to teaching and organising learning. It also explores personalised learning, effective communication with learners and how to make the most of presentation, demonstration, group learning, individualised instruction and teaching on line. To support this it explores using new technologies and social networks to engage and motivate learners.

Introduction

Most teachers suggest that there are two essential ingredients for successful learning: motivation (or wanting to learn) and making sense of (or digesting) the learning experience. Brilliant teaching means creating effective learning environments. Environments where learners are actively participating and engaged with the material are vital to learning. Learners need to be engaged and motivated to learn. People learn by actively participating and engaging in a number of ways, which includes observing, speaking, writing, listening, thinking, partaking and doing. Learning can be improved when a person sees potential implications, applications, and benefits to others. Importantly, learning builds on current understanding, practices and knowledge.

Approaches to engaging learners and designing for a variety of styles and experience

Learning styles

Learning styles are an important aspect of learning that are useful to factor into your teaching and learning strategies. If everyone learned the same way, it would be easy to choose teaching strategies to optimise learning. How people learn, however, varies widely, as does individual preference for receiving and processing information.

Most people are predominantly one type of learner, but usually they can adapt to another style. Learners do tend to look for their preferred style in each learning situation because they associate that style with learning success.

Visual learners

Visual learners are those who generally think in pictures. They often prefer to see things written down in a hand-out, text, on a PowerPoint, Prezi or other visual medium. They find graphs, charts, and other visual learning tools to be extremely effective. They remember things best by seeing something.

Auditory learners

Auditory learners are those who generally learn best by listening. They typically like to learn through lectures, discussions, and reading aloud. They remember best through hearing or saying things aloud.

Kinesthetic learners

Kinesthetic, also called tactile, learners are those who learn best through touching, feeling, and experiencing that which they are trying to learn. They remember best by writing or physically manipulating the information.

Environmental learners

They process new information best when it is presented in surroundings that match learner preferences (room temperature, aesthetics, lighting, seating, etc.).

Reflection and activity

Consider your own teaching styles and how you prefer to be taught.

While most individuals can learn using any one of the afore-mentioned styles, most people have one which they prefer, as you may have identified from your own reflections. Remember when considering learning styles and your class:

- Learning styles will vary in your class. Consider your own learning styles; they may be the same as or different even from your learners.
- What works well for you may not work well for some of your learners. Because each of us knows what works for ourselves, we can have the tendency to select teaching strategies that favour our own learning styles. If you choose only teaching strategies that would optimise learning for learners with your learning styles, many of the learners in your class may be at a disadvantage.
- Knowing something about learning styles in general and your own learning styles in particular can help you to plan and deliver the teaching and learning strategies that reach learners with as many different learning styles as possible. Teaching for young people and adult learners will incorporate presentation methods to engage as many of these styles as possible, to be effective for a group of diverse participants.

Being aware of learning styles can help you develop inclusive lessons that take regard of a rich and diverse learner group. This diversity may include ethnicity, gender, age, cultural background, etc. The diversity of the learners can impact on the classroom in many ways, which includes the diversity of the learning styles of your learners.

Personalised learning

Truly personalised learning means that we are enabling all learners, whatever their starting point, to fulfil their potential. Personalised learning is a shared process involving teachers and individual learners. Personalised learning recognises that learners initiate their learning experience/journey from different starting points and that they possess unique aptitudes, capacities, socially situated knowledge and skills that may not have been previously recognised or used to best effect to overcome barriers to learning. Pedagogy for personalisation includes initial and diagnostic assessment based on what learners know and want to know.

Initial assessment happens at the time of a learner's transition into a new learning programme. It is a holistic process, during which you start to build up a picture of an individual's achievements, skills, interests, previous learning experiences and goals, and the learning needs associated with those goals. This information is used as a basis for negotiating a course or programme.

Diagnostic assessment helps to identify specific learning strengths and areas for development. It determines learning targets and appropriate teaching and learning strategies to achieve them. This is important because many learners have higher-level skills in some areas than in others. Diagnostic assessment happens initially at the beginning of a learning programme and subsequently when the need arises. It is related to specific skills needed for tasks.

The two processes of initial and diagnostic assessment are interconnected, the diagnostic assessment adding to the information gathered from initial assessment.

Together they help build a clear picture of the individual in order to:

- personalise learning
- develop an individual learning plan (ILP)
- begin the process of assessment for learning that will continue throughout the learner's programme
- make links to progression routes and prepare for the next steps in the learner's journey.

So, what is an Individual Learning Plan?

The ILP plays an essential role in ensuring that the assessment outcomes inform teaching and learning. The ILP steers the learning journey, informed by the outcomes of assessment at various stages in that journey. An ILP should include topics such as:

- What am I doing? What are the next steps?
- What have I achieved/gained? Where do I want to go?
- What skills/knowledge do I need to develop to get there?

Points to be considered when using an ILP with your learners include the following:

- Involve your learners in taking an active part in their ILP. Use learners' own knowledge of their strengths and development needs to set learning targets meaningful to them.
- Ensure there is a link between the learning targets on the ILP and teaching and learning taking place.
- Work with the learner to keep the ILPs updated by reviewing progress regularly.

ILPs are an excellent tool for learners to be actively involved in their learning. This participation and ownership can be both motivational and empowering for learners.

Communication

Effective communication is an essential part of great teaching. The quality and effectiveness of such communication have a lot to do with the amount and quality of learning that takes place. The basic principles of teaching relate to effective communication and should be visible within a lesson plan. Communication means the whole environment of effective teaching as well as simply verbal speaking and listening by the learner and teacher.

Verbal communication

No matter how well the tables and chairs are arranged in the class, a teacher who mumbles to the board, who speaks in a monotone manner without enthusiasm, who uses unexplained technical and specialist terms, who does not repeat points and speaks too quickly, is much less effective. In the classroom situation, the teacher's skilful use of language cannot be over-emphasised. This is what is referred to as style. The quality of style can be termed good, weak or indifferent depending on the linguistic choices of the speaker (do they use subject-specific meta-language without defining it first?) and the manner in which the words chosen are woven together to function in connected speech. Therefore, the teacher should choose an accessible and meaningful style of speech, which will assist in getting the students to understand certain concepts and ideas, and to remember the lesson content. Implementing subject-specific meta-language acquisition into your lessons can be very empowering and motivational for your learners. A way to do this is to identify the subject-specific terminology you are going to use in the lesson (which can often be a barrier for many learners) and build class activities which facilitate the learners' awareness of the words, what they mean and how they are applied. This could be actioned through the use of word quizzes, word definition sheets, etc. Learners can then develop confidence and ease in applying the meta-language to their assignment, verbal discussion and on their trajectory into employment and/or further study.

Listening

Listening is a major factor in participating in the teaching/learning process. Listening involves much more than learning the sounds of speech. When a voice is clear and strong enough to be heard by students, their attention can more easily be held than when a voice is a whisper and incomprehensible unless you are within arm's distance of the teacher. A lesson should include language which is vivid and evokes images of experience, objects and events. To keep the interest of the learners, use intonation and let your voice move through a range of changes in pitches, loudness, and rate. The non-verbal aspects of lesson delivery such as body movements and gestures should support what you are saying to further reinforce meaning. No matter which type of presentation you decide upon using, its success will depend upon good speaking abilities and skills. To improve your presentation skills, use a well-modulated tone that makes it easy to listen to you. Speak clearly at a pace that others understand. Speaking too quickly or slowly can lose the interest of your learners and cause confusion.

Non-verbal communication

When we communicate with other people, usually in oral communication situations, there are non-verbal signals which accompany our words that would trigger meanings in the minds of receivers. These non-words, which may communicate, include objects, actions, gestures, colour, space and time. Non-verbal behaviour often complements verbal communication. In the classroom, the teacher's mode of dress, their facial expression, eye contact, bodily movements, and voice quality are those non-verbal aspects of lesson delivery that would complement verbal messages.

Effective presentations

It is not only our communication skills that make us a brilliant teacher but the way we organise the material we are going to communicate about. An important element of communication in teaching is the use of teaching aids. We have all heard the saying: 'What I hear, I forget; what I see, I remember; what I do, I know'. Pictures, written posters and practical demonstrations improve communication and we should use them as much as possible. Most of us have access to paper, posters, a whiteboard or smart board. We can use these to prepare aids for our lessons: summaries of important facts, or pictures and diagrams. Whatever your choice, it is important to organise your material so it can be readily digestible for your learners.

Organise your material in a logical order

The more organised you are as the teacher the easier it will be for others to learn from you. A way to organise information is to start with the beginning information, proceed through the middle, and conclude with the end. However, this may not be the easiest way for the learners to learn your material. There are different ways to logically organise your material for presentation.

Content sequence

Look at your content and see how the concepts/ideas/knowledge are built. Which ideas are foundational and which ideas are built on the foundation? The foundational material should be presented first to allow the learners to create their own foundation as building blocks for later material. It can be helpful in your planning to start by thinking through the concluding ideas that you want your learners to understand. Once you clearly understand how you will be concluding your presentation you can then work backwards until you uncover each previous idea. When you get all the way back to the beginning you are ready to begin.

Experience sequence

If you know something about the background of the young people and the adults who are attending your lessons you may also know the sorts of experiences they have had that relate to the content of your lesson. Start your planning by identifying their relevant experiences and then building on them. Present your content in an order which begins by clearly linking what you have to say/present to their own experiences and socially situated knowledge.

Interest sequence

Establish the most interesting things you have to share and then organise your presentation to allow these interesting aspects to intermittently emerge. For example, if you would like to get their interest at the beginning of the presentation make sure to start out with something that will capture their interest. Any time there is a break in the lesson and it is time to get started again, you can probably use a high interest item to get them back and tuned in again.

Reflection and activity

Identify any further strategies for delivering effective presentations.

Some key points for making your presentations sparkle include the following:

- The material presented must be intended for direct and immediate application in order to keep your learners' interest. Begin with ideas and concepts familiar to the learners as a first step to the new ideas you plan to teach.
- Keep the learners actively involved, speak with them not to them.
- Utilise a variety of training methods to vary the presentation of information and support learners' understanding of the meaning of the new knowledge or skills.

- Encourage them to share ideas and information. Involve learners in sharing what they know; build on what they know. Validate their expertise.
- Explain the information and encourage and answer questions.
- Get feedback, reinforcing the positive and redirecting the negative.
- Give learners feedback on their progress.
- Provide opportunities to practise what is learned to assist deep learning (e.g. role-plays or simulations).
- Use technology effectively, for example, PowerPoint, Prezi and blogs.
- Create illustrations/diagrams of key concepts.
- Illustrate with a case study or practical examples.
- Prepare supplementary handouts.

Group learning

Drawing on a range of theories and strategies, Jaques (2000) illustrates how the benefits of group work can be employed to enhance learning. He demonstrated how small group discussion supports learners to express themselves in their subject and to establish a closer relationship with their teacher. It also supported the development of listening, presenting ideas, arguing a case and working as a member of a team. He further suggested that it provides the opportunity for people to monitor their own learning and so gain self-direction and independence in their studies.

Reflection and activity

Consider the benefits of group learning in your classroom.

You may have identified that group work, which includes projects and tasks, can support learners' development of skills and knowledge specific to collaborative efforts, allowing them to:

- tackle more complex problems than they could on their own
- delegate roles and responsibilities – develop team working skills
- share diverse perspectives – gain an awareness of diverse view points

- pool knowledge and skills
- support one another and be accountable as a team
- receive social support and encouragement to take risks
- develop new approaches to resolving differences
- establish a shared identity with other group members
- find effective peers to be role models
- develop their own voice and perspectives in relation to peers – become empowered and be empowering.

Individualised instruction

Regardless of how hard teachers work, it is difficult for them to provide one-to-one instruction. As I am sure you will be aware or have experienced, many teachers are dealing with larger class sizes now more than ever before. In addition, they are required to ensure that every student is being taught at her or his appropriate instructional level and that all of the instruction meets the necessary standards for their particular level and awarding body.

Individualised instruction is a method of instruction in which content, instructional materials, instructional media, and pace of learning are based upon the abilities and interests of each individual learner. Individualised instruction is not the same as a one-to-one student/teacher ratio or one-to-one tutoring, as it may seem. This would be an impossible ask for most providers of education.

One of the main challenges is for teachers to offer every student this individualised instruction, including support for areas of development or enrichment.

Reflection and activity

Consider how you can implement individualised instruction into your classes.

You may have identified how effective, individualised instruction for learner achievement could include the following:

- Learners are assessed on a formative basis throughout the year.
- Appropriate instruction is assigned and delivered immediately upon completion of the assessment.

- Assignments are right at the students' point of instructional need.
- Assignments are engaging and provide personalised support, tutorials and opportunities for application.
- Assignments contain embedded assessments to determine the point of mastery so students can move forward.
- Data is available for teachers to track student progress.

The quality of the teaching materials becomes extremely important when individualised instruction is being used. Materials need to be of exceptional quality, fully explaining the content to be learned. This allows the learner to move at her or his own pace more easily since she or he doesn't need to rely as much on explanations from the lessons (although these are important). It also frees much of the teacher's time from lectures so that she or he is able to spend most of the time monitoring learners' progress and assisting those who need it. This facilitates bespoke support based on the progress of the learner.

The use of individualised instruction can also meet individual learner needs by allowing content to be diverse and varied to a certain extent, according to the interests and strengths of the learner. Once basic required content has been learned, individuals can be free to pursue additional learning within the subject according to their interests.

New technologies

With the arrival of technology across all fields of learning, the ways in which learners store and retrieve information for further use have dramatically changed. As such, multimedia, interactive technologies and new ways of developing collaboration are approaches which can be successfully utilised for learning. Ingle and Duckworth (2013) note how the focus on technology for learning is becoming an ever louder voice in the conversation on pedagogy and educational practice. Driven by social and technological changes, it is clear that economic implications are also having a significant impact on strengthening the focus for finding technological solutions to a learner and more cost-effective educational landscape. Larger class sizes, smaller budgets, learners as consumers, finding more effective ways of learning and the true globalisation of education are all contributory factors to the ongoing dialogue on the impact of technology-mediated learning. We need to ensure we keep up-to-date with technology and embed it into our lessons in creative and innovative ways that inspire and motivate our learners.

Reflection and activity

Below teacher and media specialist Dan Atkinson considers the ways blogs (short for web-logs) and social media can be used to promote engagement and learner participation. Blogs are websites where users can quickly and easily create written content to share with the world. Users add 'posts' to their developing blogs which can be viewed and commented upon. Blog narrative can be supplemented by a range of multi-media resources such as audio and video to make blogs more rich and interactive.

My professional career began in the film and television industry working as a video editor. I moved into education initially as a media technician before training to become a teacher where my subject specialism is BTEC vocational courses in Media Production at level 2, 3 and 4.

Since September (2012) I have implemented the use of online blogging and social media to improve teaching and learning. The majority of my research was based on a case study of a year two learner studying on the level 3 BTEC. This learner had spent a year without blogging and a term with the blogs so it was important to compare the quality and quantity of work. The previous year this learner had collated her work in the forms of essays, pre-production folders and portfolios. Her work, which covered 10 units, was at the high end of the merit grading criteria. Her practical work was always very creative, well planned and researched; however her written work was often hit and miss – incoherent, inarticulate and often rambling. Since the introduction of Tumblr (online blogging site) Courtney herself confesses her love for it. *'It's easier because all your work is in one place which means I don't have to remember where I've saved it. This makes it easier at home because it's all online I don't need to remember to bring a pen when I drive into college.'* What Courtney says here is important. Tumblr is alleviating certain college stresses and obstacles that appear when learners forget work or feel overwhelmed with the responsibility of organising themselves for college. In another interview Courtney went on to say that *'the feedback I receive can often be instantaneous. I'll be posting things on my blog and if the teacher is logged on they reply straight away and tell me whether I'm doing things right'*. This immediate feedback is exactly what I wanted from the online blogs. It is constant formative assessment.

Courtney's written work has certainly improved. Mainly this seems to be due to the fact that she writes little and often now. Courtney posts small blog entries of around 150–300 words which often include pictures, video or links to research. Having the burden of a 1500 word essay clearly affected her writing and this development has indeed improved her grade. The one variable might be that as Courtney is now a second year she has matured somewhat and is therefore more capable of producing elucidated written work, however Courtney disagrees with this: *'visually it feels like you don't have to do as much, but I am actually achieving more'*.

The blogging process is successful because it does away with the traditional essay writing, hand-in, marking procedure that teachers and learners have to endure and in its place creates a learning relationship between teacher and learner that is more fluid, efficient and productive. I now embed blogging and other social media tools into my lessons to inspire, motivate and make learning great for the learners.

Encouraging your learners to get blogging can also be a great way to develop literacy skills and encourage creative, factual or critical writing. The online written format can encourage many non-traditional learners to express themselves, creating tangible evidence for assessment. Blogging can also be used to encourage reflective practice, perhaps during a group project, when creating an event or throughout a study process. By responding to other learners' posts, learners can enter a dialogue and demonstrate their critical reasoning skills. And for you, creating your own blog is a great way to share information, links and the latest subject-specific news to your blog followers which may be your peers or wider interest group.

To create a blog you can visit the following websites:

Wordpress   www.wordpress.com
Blogger   www.blogger.com
Tumblr   www.tumblr.com
Posterous   www.posterous.com

ICT tools

ICT tools can be used to find, explore, analyse, exchange and present information in a creative way. To be most effective your Internet activities should be fun, engaging, and educational. Regardless of age, interests, abilities, and disabilities, all learners should actively participate. Tools you may want to use include:

- **Animoto** (www.animoto.com) is an online service to create videos from images.

   You could use a video made by yourself to bring your subject specialism alive and/or encourage your learners to create a video to strengthen their knowledge.
- **Twitter** (www.twitter.com) is a tool that allows you to stay in touch and keep up with colleagues and students no matter where you are or what you're doing. You could use twitter to email learners with feedback or extended activities to develop independent study.
- **Bubbl-us** (http://bubbl.us/) is a mindmapping application that lets you brainstorm online. You could use this to explore your and your learners' thoughts on particular areas/aspects they are studying. It is an excellent strategy for encouraging the flow of ideas, debate and critical thinking.
- **QR codes are 2D bar codes.** A QR codes might sound scarily complicated – they did to me at first – but they're surprisingly easy to use and can be an informative and fun addition to the classroom. If you're not familiar with QR codes, they are black and white pictures (similar to the barcodes that appear on items of food, etc.). The information stored on them varies from text, phone number, messages to be sent through SMS, and URLs. Using compatible software on a compatible mobile phone (at least with camera), the QR codes can display text to the

users, auto-dial a phone call, auto-send an SMS, or auto-open a specific webpage for the users.

You could use QR codes to get student feedback in class. For example, you could ask students in closed-questions (for example, yes/no) by letting students scan the appropriate QR code (either the Yes or No QR code). This would send a pre-written SMS message to the SMS service that you can access to get the results via a web page.

You can generate your own QR codes, using a website such as QRStuff at: http://www.qrstuff.com/, and put them in work-sheets, in emails and online.

- **Prezi** (http://prezi.com/) is a great communication tool that helps you communicate, present and share the content of your lesson. It is a good way of stepping beyond what many learners consider boring PowerPoint slides and delivering a dynamic and creative presentation to hold the learners' interest.

Reflection and activity

How and when could you use an ICT tool in your class?

Choose an ICT tool from above and create a resource for a future lesson.

Once delivered reflect on the impact of the ICT tool on learning.

Embedding technology

You can embed ICT into your specialist area as a means to assist learners to achieve both standards in ICT and their specialism. Used well, ICT is also a powerful motivator for many 'hard to reach learners' and linking the subjects can encourage many learners to participate. Mellar et al. (2007) suggest that:

- ICT is a powerful tool to raise levels of literacy and numeracy.
- Computers and multimedia software provide attractive ways of learning.
- The web enables access to the best materials and the most exciting learning opportunities.

- ICT offers a new start for adults returning to learning.
- The internet and digital TV technology can reach into the home.
- Learners who use ICT for basic skills double the value of their study time, acquiring two sets of skills at the same time.

Reflection and activity

Consider how you can embed ICT into your lessons.

Now read teacher educators Dawne Bell and David Wooff's, approaches to using Technology Enhanced Learning (TEL) to increase engagement and improve attainment.

This short case study seeks to illustrate how, when used as a delivery tool for teaching, the utilisation and creative deployment of new technologies can enhance learning. Also when used thoughtfully, technology can have a significant impact upon improving pupils' and learners' engagement, learning experience and subsequently their academic attainment.

Here we describe how final year undergraduate trainees, studying to become qualified teachers, used Technology Enhanced Learning (TEL) not only to help them learn, but through modelling TEL as an effective mode of delivery, trainees were encouraged to realise the potential of this approach to engage the pupils and learners they will subsequently teach.

The work in this particular study built upon the notion of 'Design Fiction' (Sterling 2005) as a catalyst for the trainees 'futuristic' design work, and was employed initially in order to reflect the content which was being delivered. Previously this work involved the production of a traditional paper-based design portfolio and three-dimensional solid block model, and existing delivery strategies included traditional taught sessions and small group seminars, individual tutorials, practical workshop demonstrations and the production and presentation of module outcomes via sketch book and folio work and prototype models. The TEL strategies and approaches were introduced in addition to the traditional modes of study already in existence and included the employment of the enhanced use of the virtual learning environment, QR Codes, Prezi™, Blogs and Augmented Reality.

For those trainees who expressed a desire to engage with the TEL initiative, specifically the new approaches included the enhanced use of the virtual learning environment and the use of 'blogging' as an alternative to the production of a traditional paper-based design portfolio. Supplemental work engaged a significant number of trainees in the generation and utilisation of QR Codes to explore and aid the visual communication of their design concepts and decisions to others.

The effect amongst the group was contagious, and yielded tangible outcomes that had a series of positive impacts on attainment, motivation and engagement.

The use of Prezi™ was employed to enhance lesson delivery as opposed to PowerPoint style presentations; blogging was used with older pupils in order to develop electronic design portfolios. The enhanced use of QR codes was used to support learning in numerous ways, including enabling pupils to access video demonstrations of tools, equipment and skills outside of taught lessons, and to deliver audio files for use with groups of pupils with specific special educational learning needs.

Where trainees used blogging, engagement was increased and tutors were able to view and comment on individual trainee development virtually, which reduced the need for formal tutorials. The use of the blog, for those working in this way, replaced the need to create a paper-based design portfolio and tutors also noted increased levels of communication between trainees. In viewing each other's work and progress an informal system of 'interactive peer assessment' developed which led to increased levels of self-reflection on a much more regular basis than previously acknowledged by trainees. In turn trainees reported that they felt it had impacted significantly upon the quality of the work they produced.

Via the developed use of the blog, trainees were able to produce 'living' design portfolios, while through the use of Prezi™ they were able to create dynamic teaching resources.

The use of virtual learning spaces, and also the potential benefits of integrating mixed and augmented realities to support the creation of subject-specific three-dimensional artefacts for use in the classroom had a significant positive impact.

A number of trainees referred specifically to the 'competitive element', which had been inadvertently introduced through the use of blogging, and several cited their increased engagement and motivation in part as being due to being able to see how much progress was being made by their peers. Sharing ideas, resources and research was also cited as a distinct benefit.

For those trainees with their own specific learning needs, they reported that the use of the blog and the other TEL strategies helped to increase their confidence, which they attributed to their ability to record their learning as it developed, not via written explanations and paper portfolios, but through a living portfolio of video clips and audio files.

Throughout the module, tutors used an iterative approach to evaluation and feedback from trainees with respect to the implementation of TEL. Regular feedback was gained from trainees to ensure that they were able to understand the implementation of TEL within the module and to ensure that the pace of technological utilisation was suitable for all learners.

Fundamentally the initial intervention, which sought to explore the tangible benefits gained through the adoption of working with TEL, was academic in origin. However following completion of the module, a number of the trainees then proceeded to adopt aspects of their work and integrated a number of the TEL-based strategies whilst on their teaching placements. Trainees found that in using TEL to enhance the delivery of lessons, the engagement of pupils was increased and it had a positive impact upon levels of attainment. Innovative ideas employed by trainees included the development of resources for differentiation, particularly EAL and subject specific Phonics, instructional videos and homework tasks.

Technology is constantly developing and evolving, and it is important to remember that in twelve or eighteen months' time the technology will have moved forward, and what is cutting edge now won't be then.

It is also important to remember that because of its nature, many aspects of the technology we have discussed here are 'novel' and care must be taken to avoid the overuse, or the inappropriate use of technology. Technology enhanced learning is Not A Gimmick (NAG) and its use as such must be avoided. So while we do not wish to 'NAG' you, please only use technology if it enhances the learning and if it doesn't enhance then don't use it.

Final thoughts

The key to teaching young people and adults is to understand how they learn. This means placing emphasis on your learners' needs and having insights, creativity and skills when planning great lessons. Being aware of the practices our learners bring into the classroom and shaping our lesson to respond to them is essential. For example, use new and emerging technologies in innovative and meaningful ways that enthuse digitally engaged learners to go that extra mile. The lessons should also promote learners to view one another as resources and value and share their world picture, knowledge and skills. Mutual respect, trust, comfort, collaboration, and freedom to participate should characterise productive and empowering learning environments where great learning and teaching flourishes.

Further reading

Hill, C. (2007) *Teaching with e-learning in the Lifelong Learning Sector (Achieving QTLS)*, 2nd edn. Exeter: Learning Matters.

Ingle, S. and Duckworth, V. (2012) *Enhancing Learning through Technology in Lifelong Learning: Fresh ideas; innovative strategies.* Maidenhead: Open University Press.

Turnbull, J. (2007) *The 9 Habits of Highly Effective Teachers: A Practical Guide to Personal Development*, London: Continuum.

Websites

Teaching styles questionnaire: www.geoffpetty.com/
Association of Learning Technology (ALT): www.alt.ac.uk
The Association for Information Technology in Teacher Education (ITTE): www.itte.org.uk
JISC: www.jisc.ac.uk
The ICT Association (NAACE): www.naace.co.uk
JISC VITAL: www.vital.ac.uk
Futurelab: www.futurelab.org.uk

Chapter 6

How will I keep their interest?

The objectives of this chapter

This chapter explores approaches to engaging students and designing for a variety of styles and experience. To do this it looks at the organisation where teaching takes place, our own practical learning, learning at work, activity in learning and problem-based learning. It also explores action learning as a development tool.

Introduction

As a teacher, working in a team is an important part of your own learning. Few of us work as lone practitioners and understanding our situation as a teacher is almost inevitably a matter of thinking about how we relate to others. To begin to think about this we need to understand the organisation we work in and the impact this has on us as teachers.

Reflection and activity

To help gain a clearer understanding of the context in which your teaching is taking place, reflect on and note down:

- how your college or centre is structured and why
- what effect the structure has on your work
- how you are managed and developed as a member of staff.

The organisation in which you work

The aims of this section are:

- to develop a critical awareness of how teaching and learning organisations are structured both formally (in other words, what they are meant to be) and informally (in other words, how they operate in practice)
- to evaluate how workplace culture and practice will influence your role as a teacher
- to consider the knowledge, understanding and skills requirements for being a fantastic FE teacher in different organisations and institutions.

Images and organisations

Think of one of your first encounters as a trainee teacher employee with your organisation. Reflect on a time when you had little experience of working in your organisation and you were coming in with an open mind and open eyes. This may be a recent event or some time ago.

Consider:

- What was it like, what did the first encounter feel like? Were you formally inducted, introduced, what do you think it was supposed to feel like?
- Try to recall an incident, a conversation, an observation, an event which captures what it is really like working for that organisation.
- Make notes of how you felt at that time.
- Now look at the language you have used and what you have said. What does this tell you about the organisation, its structure and culture?
- Did the above match the formal description or view of organisation, structure and culture?

Review your findings and consider whether they have implications for your role as a teacher. Is the organisation's formal response to teachers' and students' needs likely to be different from reality?

Structures and organisations

Now think how your organisation sees itself and promotes itself. How is it structured formally? Can you describe its formal structure? Is the authority represented in this formal structure challenged in any way? Can you give examples of this? To what extent does the formal structure accurately reflect the real power and behaviour in the organisation? Is it possible to replace the formal designed structure with a more accurate diagram? If not, then why not?

Developing insight into the organisation in which you work

- Produce a formal structure diagram for your organisation as a whole and for your department.
- Review how close these structures are to the reality of work and organisation within your workplace.
- Design a departmental structure chart which accurately reflects behaviour in your department.

The focus of the exercise is a critical analysis of workplace structures by addressing the concept of the informal structure *versus* the corporate structure – what happens as opposed to what is supposed to happen. Reflect on the difficulty in completing this task, identifying issues of confidentiality, language and allegiances.

Again, consider the implications of an organisation which is committed to learning and the interests of students.

- How will your findings impact on your analysis of workplace practice?
- Does your organisational structure permit reflective analysis which may lead to criticism and suggestions for improvement?
- How involved/interested will your line manager be in your role?

You as a human resource

Think of your career to date. How have you arrived where you are? Has this come about from a process of careful planning and career management? If so, what strategies did you use? How are your professional and work needs dealt with?

Considering how you are managed as a 'human resource':

- critically review your job description or that of a teacher for those of you on teaching placement;
- write your 'real' job description for your current post, as opposed to the formal description;
- review how you are supported in your work through formal and informal support mechanisms. Are you managed in a 'supportive/non-supportive' manner?
- how involved is your college/centre in encouraging and supporting a strategy for career development?

From your analysis, consider how much what you actually do day by day is relevant to your actual or 'real' job description.

Planning for the future

Your reading resource for this section should be documents or directives your organisation has produced about future strategy.

Having thought about how your organisation works, and how you are managed within it, consider what you know about your organisation's plans for the future. What extra knowledge and skills need to be brought into the workplace to enable it to meet its plans? How is your organisation proposing to manage changes in the knowledge and skills which underpin its work?

- From organisational and departmental documents, and discussions with your workplace colleagues/peers, identify how what you do can integrate with the development needs of the workplace. What is of particular value in your subject context?
- What particular development needs have been identified for you through formal organisational activities such as appraisal or informal conversations with workplace colleagues and people with management responsibility?
- Looking at your sector of work and personal career strategy, what is required to develop you as an individual with the necessary knowledge and skills to meet your work aspirations and deal with changes in your sector?

SWOT analysis

Having reviewed your organisation, its development plans and your role within its development, carry out the 'SWOT' exercise to analyse strengths, weaknesses, opportunities and threats in the context of your organisation.

- Can you identify the knowledge and skills which your workplace should be developing?
- Do your views on this matter correspond with those of your college/centre?
- What knowledge and skills are appropriate to your subject area of study?

The learning process at work

Using the workplace as a learning resource

We now move on to look at the way in which people learn at work and how we can structure 'learning by doing' within an academic programme of study.

As anyone involved in education knows, **activity** is an important element in the process of learning. We master a skill or come to understand a new idea by doing something with it. This may be repetitive practice, something physical and direct, or it may be the application of an idea or theory to an actual case.

Most of us will have learned how to change gear in a car by repetitive practice, while our mathematical knowledge will probably have been developed through applying principles to actual cases (e.g. testing out 'circumference = $2\pi r$' by measuring actual circles). In both these cases, we could memorise rules or theories but real personal learning only began when we started to apply the knowledge we had acquired.

This principle that the best teaching and the most effective learning involve *learning by doing* is at the heart of much educational theory and is a central tenet of this book. Practical activity provides a good focus for learning because it is a context in which people can put theories and principles directly into operation, utilising real problems, processes and issues.

It is also a place where new information is created through the implementation of knowledge, skills and ideas in each unique situation. In this book you will be required to consider how better use can be made of your practical experience and knowledge through linking activity to reflection.

Activity as a learning resource

The aim of this section is to encourage you to see activity as the key learning resource and to help you to consider how we can draw on activities in classrooms, workshops or the workplace in much the same way as more conventional courses draw on material from a library.

Experiential learning

Learning by doing is often described as experiential learning, i.e. learning from the experiences we meet with as we go through our lives. This could make it seem as if the learning process was simply a matter of getting on with things and that anyone who had had a lot of experiences had automatically learned a lot. Yet most of us know people who never change or develop however much happens to them. Some people could be regarded as impervious to experience.

In fact it seems that people only learn from their experiences if they *reflect* on what happens to them. When we are at work, we carry out the same routine very often without thinking, and generally without learning anything about the process.

This unreflective activity is unlikely to lead us to develop our skills or attitudes. Sometimes, when something about the task or process surprises us (the machine breaks down, a new staff member asks a question), we stop to think. It is in this situation that learning is likely to take place.

Problem-based learning

Based on constructivist theories brought forward by theorists such as Vygotsky and Dewey (1910), problem-based learning (PBL) is much more student-centred than traditional teacher-led approaches. PBL requires the teacher to play the facilitator while these learning projects are going on. The motivations and drive may begin with a problem.

In education there has been a historical divide between theory and practice, for example, theory has to be learned prior to dealing with practice. Problem-based learning (PBL) subverts this divide. Problems stemming from practice are used as prompts to acquire theoretical knowledge.

In PBL, learners use 'triggers' from the problem case or scenario to define their own learning objectives. Subsequently they do independent, self-directed study before returning to the group to discuss and refine their acquired knowledge. In a problem-based learning model, students engage complex, challenging problems and collaboratively work toward their resolution. PBL is about students connecting disciplinary knowledge to real-world problems. The motivation to solve a problem becomes the motivation to learn.

Reflection and activity

> Consider what you already know/do not know about PBL.

You may have identified that PBL may have a content of:

- the scenario/case study
- the problem
- the context/situation
- the knowledge
- the skills
- the attitudes/beliefs/values

while the process may include:

- talking
- dialogue
- questioning
- hypothesising
- collaboration
- activity
- communication skills
- interpersonal skills.

The method can be summarised in the following fashion:

1. Students are split into groups and the **problem** is presented to the group.
2. The group will then pick out and organise the **facts** of the problem.
3. The group will then formulate their **ideas** as to how best to research solutions.
4. The group will identify the **learning needs**, in other words, what the group needs to learn in order to solve the problem.
5. The group will then **share the findings of their research** and reflect on the work performed.

One of the arguments used to support the superiority of PBL is the concept of contextual learning. The basic premise is that when we learn material in the context of how it will be used, it promotes learning and the ability to use the information. In PBL, the problem is usually portrayed in the real-life context of a patient coming to visit a doctor, for example.

PBL can be very challenging to implement, as it requires a lot of planning and hard work for the teacher. I would suggest that PBL needs to be well defined and integrated into your curriculum area. It also needs to be organised well and the learners need to understand what it is, for example, they need to learn about the process of learning. It is a very motivational way for learners to learn and most really enjoy the collaborative and interactive approach. It offers learners a space for them to speak about the topics raised and identifies solutions from their own experiences. The sharing of problems and solutions can be very rewarding and motivational.

Criticisms

One common criticism of PBL is that students cannot really know what might be important for them to learn, especially in areas which they have no prior experience. Therefore teachers, as facilitators, must be careful to assess and account for the prior knowledge that learners bring to the educational setting.

Reflection and activity

Below Dawne Bell considers PBL in the curriculum area of Design and Technology. Identify any aspects of her approach that you could apply to your own practice.

Within the curriculum area of Design and Technology the concept of Problem-Based Learning (PBL) is an approach which has long been embedded.

In essence PBL is a research-based method of learning, where pupils, students or in this case study trainee teachers are encouraged, through 'real world applications' to solve problems. Where content or material is not merely learnt by rote, but through the active employment of contextual learning it promotes the learners' ability to actually use what is learnt by putting it into practice.

Specifically within Design and Technology, learners are encouraged to use knowledge and facts acquired in other curriculum areas, for example, science and maths, and apply them to solve practical problems, which in this context are to design and make products and systems that meet human needs.

This short case study seeks to illustrate how, through engagement with PBL, undergraduate trainees studying to become qualified teachers of Design and Technology, used PBL not only to help them learn, but through modelling it as a delivery mode, to enable them to recognise the power of this approach as a tool via which they can engage pupils they subsequently teach.

PBL adopts an approach which moves away from traditional 'teacher-led' modes of delivery, to one in which the student acquires problem-solving skills for themselves. So learners are not just trained to recall knowledge and facts, but they begin to develop a deeper understanding of how and when to apply them and in doing so learn to think creatively, and begin to solve problems both as individuals, and as members of a team.

These problems can be either theoretical or practical, but in this study the task was of a practical nature.

Building upon content (fact and knowledge) which had been delivered in a 'traditional' way (via teacher-led input and a series of practical demonstrations) over two sessions, the undergraduate trainees were set a challenge which required them to take an active part in their own learning. The set design brief required them not only to recall the knowledge they had learnt, and practise the skills they had been shown, but to demonstrate how what they had been taught could be applied in practice to solve a 'real life' design problem.

So rather than being 'taught' in the formal sense, during this phase of the learning, as is often associated with PBL, small groups of students began to work together.

It was made clear to trainees at this point that the tutor would now become a facilitator, in place to support the work, and would no longer be 'leading' the lessons.

Trainees were able to 'self-select' their groups, and became responsible for organising and managing their time, resources and if appropriate the allocation of roles for each team member. They were encouraged to discuss their findings with their peers, and in doing so were encouraged to take a greater part in their own learning.

During the second and reflective 'prong' of this approach, trainees were encouraged to challenge their original expectations. It was apparent when the brief was introduced that whilst the majority relished the opportunity to 'get stuck in', a small number had been quite uncertain about what they had to do, and in particular a small number expressed particular concerns about 'getting it wrong'.

At this stage, with the task complete, trainees were encouraged to unpick the process and articulate how they had moved from simply practising a skill they had been shown, to be able to adapt that skill, and combine it with others, to consider the knowledge and facts they had been taught, to apply it in order to help solve the design brief, and in doing so consolidate the knowledge and really embed their understanding.

Then through evaluation and reflection, in addition to considering how they themselves had been able to embed what they had learnt in a practical way, they began to unpick the activity from the perspective of a teacher acting as a facilitator. Trainees were encouraged to consider how this kind of approach may feel to a pupil, given that a number of the group had themselves felt anxious, before moving on to consider a number of issues arising; would they allow pupils to self-select groups (if working in groups)? Is this an appropriate approach for all learners? And how could they assess an individual pupil's learning?

As a strategy PBL is an effective and powerful tool, which can be adopted for effective use with a range of learners. In this study in order to introduce PBL as a concept, the specific approach was to encourage trainees to work as a group. However it can be used as successfully for paired or individual work, depending upon the learners, learning context and desired outcome by the facilitating tutor.

Kolb and the learning cycle

It does not seem very practical to wait for the unusual to happen if we are keen to learn and develop. We need to develop an approach which gets us to 'stop and think' regularly if we are to start learning at work. The psychologist David Kolb recognises this in his model of the experiential learning cycle.

One of the most influential theories linking learning and experience was developed by David Kolb in the 1970s. What Kolb did was to set out the learning process as a cycle. He argued that it was not enough for someone to simply have experiences in order to learn. Unless we do something with our experiences they are frequently forgotten or remembered as a separate meaningless item.

What is needed is for the individual to reflect on their experience and out of this reflection come ideas and new thoughts which provide the basis for further development. Crucially reflection leads to generalisation or the production of new concepts. This ability to generalise or produce new concepts can then provide the basis for encountering new situations. We can try our new ideas out in new settings or on slightly different cases.

What this model suggests is that experience by itself, or thinking by itself is not enough. Experience and thought (reflection) need to be linked in a cycle which leads on to action or change.

David Kolb's (1984) influential experiential learning cycle is used extensively within the field of reflective practice. For Kolb, the reflective cycle can start at any stage as long as it is followed in sequence and cyclically. The core elements replicate those found in Dewey's, Schön's and Brookfield's theory (Dewey 1938, Schön

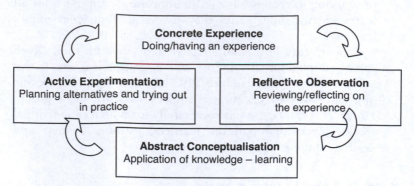

Figure 6.1 The experiential learning cycle

1983, 1987, Brookfield 1995). The process brings you back to the starting point of experience but this is approached differently in the light of what has been learned (see Figure 6.1).

So an individual learner has an experience, reflects on the experience by drawing on different perspectives and models that already exist in the mind, re-forms the ideas on the basis of this reflection, and tests out the new ideas by attempting to apply them to new experiences or situations. S/he then has a new model of practice.

Graham Gibbs (1988) gives the example of a nurse learning to lift patients by using a dummy. The first piece of supervised practice provides the *concrete experience*. Then a charge nurse might ask 'How did that feel? What might you have done differently?' to encourage *reflective observation*. That night the nurse might look up techniques and guidelines for lifting in a textbook, reading about the mechanics and physiology which underlie the practice (*abstract conceptualisation*).

Finally the nurse brings this learning to bear on a new situation, e.g. dealing with a patient on the ward. As a result of experience and reflection, s/he tries out a new approach (*active experimentation*), which gives the nurse a new experience with which to start the cycle again.

The Kolb model of learning prescribes a series of stages for learning to pass through in order to be effective. Learners may enter the cycle at any stage but they must pass through each stage in sequence.

Reflection and activity

Below Samantha Watters, a trainee teacher specialising in science and health and social care teaching, reflects on her practice. Consider how and why her reflections are driving her practice forward.

Individual target setting

My learners are all on the level 3 extended diploma course. They have or are working towards their GCSEs in maths and English. Some of my learners have English as an additional language (ASL) so I embed technical language throughout, e.g. I have provided a glossary of terms sheet which each learner has to complete in their own words to ensure greater understanding (Casey et al. 2007). I do not set individual targets for learners but differentiate them by assignment. Each assignment forms part of the overall grade of each learner. During this session I facilitated my learners to experiment and extrapolate from their own previous life experiences. This helped them realise the transferable skills they had as they progressed into the caring professions. I used Kolb's learning styles and experiential model (in Reece and Walker 2007) and reflected using the method put forward by Johns (1994), in brief, describe, reflect, influencing factors, alternative strategies and learning.

Describe

Concrete Experience – Learners were placed in groups of three and directed to provide me with a meal containing 400 calories. They were given a variety of foods and drinks, plates, cups, bowls etc. and access to calorie tables but no measuring apparatus.

Reflective Observation – After each group was satisfied, I allowed them measuring apparatus and asked them to work out the exact calorific values. They were very surprised at the results; the closest group was more than 150 calories out.

Abstract Conceptualisation – Learners decided they needed to be more accurate in their measurements and realised that patients they may deal with in work placements or future employment may also 'guestimate' values incorrectly.

Active Experience – The learners then used what they had learned to accurately measure their values and provide the correct quantities asked for.

Reflect

This observed session was great, learners were engaged and being adults all were confident that they knew what portion sizes were. There were a lot of resources involved and the session did get a bit hectic but I achieved what I wanted them to learn which was 'what you think you know and what you actually do know are completely different'. This approach to a lesson allowed the students to be influenced by what they thought a portion should look like using their existing knowledge. They then had to think how these strategies might be employed in the future when dealing with their own case studies and patients but incorporating sensitivity to their patients' feelings. Did the students learn? Yes and this approach has changed the way they may practice in future.

Influencing factors/alternative strategies

The learners were influenced by what they thought they knew and working in groups meant there was a lot of debate between the members as each had her own idea of what was correct but they had to come to a group compromise. I thought this would be a great approach to this task as I could observe them interacting and make notes on how they behaved towards each other. I could have simply sat the students down and lectured them but working in smaller groups means each student has greater input and it is unlikely that a member will be passive and not engage. Each learner is active and is learning by doing, maximising their involvement (Scales 2007).

Learning

I felt that this was a great approach, observed learning definitely took place and embedding numeracy into the session worked very well. Feedback from the students and my Subject Specific Mentor was positive and I plan to do more of this type of activity in future sessions.

Styles of learning

Kolb (1984) points out that although each of these stages is necessary, not all learners feel equally comfortable with each phase.

For some of us reflective observation is more congenial than active experimentation while others are happier dealing with concrete experiences than they are with abstract concepts. He goes on to indicate that individuals tend to fall into different 'learning styles' which reflect their preferences for different aspects of the cycle.

Convergers like the practical application of ideas (dominant ability – abstract conceptualisation and active experimentation).

Divergers have strengths in imaginative processes and in generating new ideas (dominant ability – concrete experience and reflective observation).

Assimilators like to create theoretical models and make sense of disparate evidence and ideas (dominant ability – abstract conceptualisation and reflective observation).

Accommodators have strengths in the implementation of plans or setting up experiments involving new experiences (dominant ability – concrete experience and active experimentation).

These types provide an interesting category system and it can be useful to try to assess where you and your colleagues fit. Remember that the styles can only be a question of emphasis. For learning to be effective all the elements of the cycle must be gone through regardless of your own styles and preferences.

Reflection and activity

Consider:

- how Kolb's theory compares to your own model of learning
- which quadrants of the cycle reflect your personal learning style?
- how similar are you and your colleagues in your learning styles?
- are there conclusions which can be drawn which have implications for your learning in a workplace context?

> • Can you identify a situation where you can see that
> you and your workplace colleagues followed a similar
> process to Kolb's learning cycle? Is there any area where
> you tend to take shortcuts across the cycle? Where did the
> main learning for you and your workplace take place?
> Could this be captured for future reference?

Reflection and learning

We have used the word 'reflection' to refer to the process whereby
people 'stop and think'. Donald Schön applies this idea of reflection
to a model of professional practice.

For Schön, learning through reflection on practice is not just
an optional extra for professional workers. It is quite simply part
of what it is to be a professional. He describes the professional as
a 'reflective practitioner' and the sort of cycle of learning discussed
by Kolb is at the heart of what it means to do a job in a professional way. The writings of Donald Schön have been among the
most influential sets of ideas on the relationship between learning and work during the last 20 years. Schön tries to address
precisely the question of what the relationship is between learning processes and work in a professional setting. How do people
learn to be professionals? What is there about professional
work which people need to learn and how does the learning take
place?

He is especially concerned with professions which deal with complex emotionally loaded or ethically contentious decision making.
Schön would argue that this description applies to nearly all professions. He is interested in what he calls 'the swampy lowlands' of
professional practice, i.e. areas where decisions have to be made in
complex or controversial settings such as the decision to take a
child into care, to treat a patient against their will, to suspend a
student or to assess a contractual claim. How do people learn to
make professional decisions of this sort?

Schön suggests that professionals develop a kind of 'artistry',
which he contrasts with 'technical problem solving'. These problems cannot be dealt with by applying technical formulae read from
a textbook. The professional has a built in 'repertoire' of past

examples, precedents and classic cases which is used to make judgements. Good experienced professionals may seem to act without reflection or deep thought but this is because they have accumulated sets of past experiences, reflected on and mulled over, which serve as measures and touchstones for action.

According to Schön the practice of the professional is one of continuous reflection. He identifies the phenomenon of 'reflection *in* action' where the practitioner is actually reflecting while they act, as well as different forms of 'reflection *on* action' which take place after the event. What all reflection does is to build up the professional's repertoire of models, stories, cases studies, metaphors, etc. which provide the experiential basis of expertise.

The great strength of Schön's theory is that as well as being a description of what good professional practice is like it also provides a model for how to become a good professional. As well as a theory of professional expertise, Schön also provides a model of professional learning.

Surface *versus* deep learning

Schön does, however, caution that self reflection can lead to 'surface' rather than 'deep' learning. If not adequately directed or challenged, an individual may simply reinforce and defend old habits and behaviours and the cycle becomes self-sealing. The learner fails to question underlying assumptions in any meaningful sense and the simple adaptation of an existing theory or premise may be insufficient to reach the heart of the issue or problem under review.

Working with Chris Argyris, Schön saw the answer to the self-reinforcement of single loop learning in double loop learning. In order to overcome the fact that the natural inclination of most people, particularly in the workplace, is to move rapidly through the reflection stage to more action, they proposed a second, interconnecting, loop where deep questioning of existing practice can take place.

This solution takes account of the fact that there is often a discrepancy between 'espoused theories' put forward to explain behaviour, and 'theories-in-use', the models of practice we are actually using. Double loop learning requires 'progressively more effective testing of assumptions and progressively greater learning about one's effectiveness' (Argyris and Schön 1974: 86).

Such 'deep' learning is difficult to achieve alone. Schön suggests a 'reflective practicum' where people come together to analyse an issue or problem and explore it from many different dimensions, including the individual's emotional response. Technical knowledge and skills are important, but so are skills in managing interpersonal relationships in a way that develops self-knowledge, capacity to learn, empathy with others and the ability to live with conflict.

Such reflection on practice can quickly move into difficult territory. While it may be acceptable to question whether someone had sufficient knowledge in a situation, it is often more problematic to suggest that they are taking a blinkered view or should review their approach to people management. Yet these issues are at the real heart of the matter under discussion.

Organisational culture again plays a significant part here. Argyris and Schön point out that the characteristics of workplaces are frequently to:

- define goals and try to achieve them
- maximise winning and minimise losing
- minimise generating or expressing negative feelings
- be rational.

Such a culture is likely to lead to self-sealing single loop learning, coping strategies rather than innovative approaches to practice which move an organisation forward. If experience does not automatically progress into reflective learning, then it is worth considering that reflective learning does not automatically bring about change – it may lead to conformity, rather than criticality or creativity as described by Tummons and Duckworth (2012). Each of these has its own value in the workplace, but we need to be aware, through reflection, of the reality of the course of action we are taking.

Reflection and activity

Consider:

- would you define yourself as a 'reflective practitioner'?
- how often do you question your own underlying assumptions and beliefs when dealing with a workplace issue?

- how open is your workplace to being a 'reflective practicum'?
- does reflection in your workplace lead to conformity, criticality or creativity?

Which, if any of the above, is most important?

Reflection and activity

Identify a particularly difficult issue for you or your workplace – one where there were conflicts of interest, complex ethical issues or deep emotional factors. How did you arrive at the eventual solution? Assess the relative importance of:

- knowledge
- skills
- people's personal approaches and attitudes.

Final thoughts

Action Learning is a means to empower you as a teacher and your learners. Action Learning programmes can encourage and enable learners to identify key issues that affect them and their communities in the classroom, locally and globally. It can raise awareness of and develop understandings of the contexts that surround us and the barriers that need to be addressed to move forward so that hopes and dreams can be realised. With your learners and peers you may want to develop an action learning set. An 'Action Learning Set' (ALS) is a group of between five and seven people who meet regularly to find practical ways of addressing the 'real life' challenges they face, and who support their own learning and development. Set members are encouraged to find their own solutions to challenges and issues through a structured process of insightful questioning combined with a balance of support and challenge from the group.

But it's not just a chit-chat shop; it is a practical approach to problem solving. Create a learning set in your organisation and/or community and keep a journal to capture yours and the group's insights now and in the future.

Further reading

Avis, J., Fisher, R., Thompson, R. (2010) *Teaching in Lifelong Learning.* Maidenhead: Open University Press.

Moon, J.A. (2004) *A Handbook of Reflective and Experiential Learning.* London: Routledge.

Ramazanoglu, C. & Holland, J. (2004) *Feminist Methodology Challenges and Choices.* London: Sage Publications Ltd.

Tummons, J. (2010) *Becoming a Professional Tutor in the Lifelong Learning Sector.* Exeter: Learning Matters.

Websites

Association of Teachers and Lecturers: www.atl.org.uk

City and Guilds: www.cityandguilds.com

Collaborative Action Research Network: http://www.esri.mmu.ac.uk/carnnew/

Reflective Practice. This journal, published four times a year, focuses on issues and practices in reflective teaching and learning in the classroom, workplace, and professions: http://www.tandf.co.uk/journals/titles/14623943.asp

Chapter 7

How will I know if they've learned it?

Chapter objectives

This chapter explores assessment as part of the learning process. To support this it considers effective design together with reliability and validity of assessment. Feedback and feed-forward which includes assessment as a conversation with the learner are also explored.

How will I know if they've really 'got it'?

In my teaching career I have delivered and observed dozens of peers, trainee and qualified teachers across diverse specialisms and contexts. When I finish my own class I always find it useful to ask myself 'did they get it and if not why not?' It really helps me unpick how useful the lesson's assessment strategies have been in tracking the learners' progress (or not). I tend to use a simple reflective cycle to help guide my own and the learners' thinking and find solutions to address any development areas. I have found this particularly meaningful in generating my own and the class's knowledge on strategies that we can use to improve and drive the assessment process forward. As such, after I have observed a lesson, I sit down with the teacher and ask them, 'How do you know if they got it, whether they understood and if not why not?' I have discovered they usually struggle to find a clear answer, much the same way I did when I first began asking myself the question. Some of them say it's when everyone pays attention, looks towards the whiteboard/flipchart when they deliver presentations, and the class behaviour is good. Others say it's when nobody has any questions. None of these are really good enough reasons to conclude that real learning has taken place. What I'm really trying to get at is how you can be sure they truly have really understood and 'got' what it is you are teaching them.

A great teacher is aware of their learners' progress, strengths and areas for development and plans for this. Great teaching is about ensuring learning is taking place.

Reflection and activity

Consider the ways you know your learners have understood and 'got' your lesson.

Assessment

Assessment should take place at every stage of the learning process and it should be fairly frequent. Of course, there are many different methods of assessment. So, at the start of a course some form of diagnostic assessment should take place to see how much students know. This can then be used as a type of *benchmark* used later on to see how much progress has been made.

Throughout a course various forms of assessment can be used, from question and answering strategies, homework, individual/ group project work, and in-class activities to more formal tests. If you are required to give students a certain number of tests each year, for example, four, then one thing you could do is give them six and tell them that only the best four will be used. This kind of flexibility not only helps students be less worried and anxious but also takes into account that people have bad days sometimes.

Assessment determines student approaches to learning

One of the most common questions a teacher hears from students is 'Will this be in the exams?' It is well recognised by educationalists that students are preoccupied with what constitutes the assessment in their specialist subject, so we need to recognise that assessment usually drives student learning.

If students allow assessment to define and prioritise what is central to learn, and ultimately how they spend their time learning it, then it is up to us as teachers to recognise this, and plan for it meaningfully. The methods and timing of our assessment send messages to students. As such we should take into consideration the most important areas we want our students to learn from, create clear and upfront learning outcomes, and assess appropriately. We should also be aware of the differences between 'deep' and 'surface' learning and use assessment to produce students who are deep rather than surface learners.

What kind of skills do I want students to develop?

When making your assessment plan, think about different skills and knowledge you would like your students to achieve based on the learning outcomes. Assessment should help prepare students with a wide range of transferable skills and competencies. For example, a multi-choice paper is a good way to measure and assess your students' recall skills. However, while it might be an appropriate assessment method when testing for knowledge of, say, 'the use of hair care products in a salon', it would be less appropriate to set a multi-choice task to assess whether a student had mastered a particular practical skill in hairdressing.

Main forms of assessment

Now that we have considered the broad reasons for assessment, we can explore the main forms of assessment which are:

- Initial assessment
- Diagnostic assessment
- Formative assessment
- Summative assessment
- Ipsative assessment.

Initial assessment

The initial assessment methods you use will depend on your subject area and any requirements of your organisation. It is a holistic process, during which you start to build up a picture of an individual's achievements, skills, interests, previous learning experiences and goals, and the learning needs associated with those goals. This information is used as a basis for negotiating a course or programme. Although all teachers should use some initial assessment to identify students' needs, some subjects require more stringent initial assessment. Initial assessment has always been a vital part of teaching adult basic skills (functional skills: literacy, language and numeracy) but is increasingly valued across a number of specialisms and age groups. Initial assessment helps identify a student's skills and knowledge against a level or levels within the National Standards. Students may have different levels of reading, writing, numeracy and language skills. Initial assessment is often used to help place learners in appropriate learning programmes. It is usually followed by detailed diagnostic assessment.

It is important that it is carried out in a sensitive way whereby the student feels respected and valued rather than anxious and uncomfortable. The initial assessment determines the starting point of the student. It identifies their learning and support needs and facilitates the development of an individual learning plan (see personalised approaches) which provides the framework for their learning.

Diagnostic assessment

This assessment is primarily used to identify the needs and prior knowledge of the learners for the purpose of directing them to the most appropriate learning experience.

> Identify diagnostic strategies for your specialist area/learners.

So, what happens in diagnostic assessment? Diagnostic assessments are typically used in pre-learning assessments, before a person engages in a learning experience. For example, a college student who struggles with basic skills might take an assessment to discover if his or her literacy and/or numeracy skills are of the level required for taking other courses. The assessment measures the learner's current knowledge and skill to provide feedback to help the teacher tailor the course effectively. Diagnostic assessments are used to determine knowledge and identify skills gaps and needs. In addition, this type of assessment can place students within suitable learning experiences by checking their preferred learning styles.

Formative assessment

Formative assessment emphasises the importance of actively engaging students in their own learning processes, resonates with teachers' goals for the development of students' higher-order thinking skills and skills for learning-to-learn. Formative assessment helps both learner and teacher to review progress and is a central part of the learning process. It takes place during a learning programme on a regular basis. It helps learners and their teachers to identify progress in relation to the learning objectives/plan. Progress should be recorded and new learning goals identified for the class and individuals.

Some of the most influential work on formative assessment has been carried out by Black and William (1998). 'Inside the black box: Raising standards through classroom assessment' (*Phi Delta Kappan*, October 1998) provides strong evidence from an extensive literature review to show that classroom 'formative' assessment, properly implemented, is a powerful means to improve student learning. This research indicates that improving learning through assessment depends on misleadingly simple factors:

- providing effective feedback to students
- students' active involvement in their own learning
- adjusting teaching to take into account the results of assessment
- recognising the deep influence of assessment on students' motivation and self-esteem
- ensuring students assess themselves and understand how to improve.

So what does formative assessment do? Formative assessment supports learning by generating feedback information that is of benefit to students and to teachers. Feedback on performance, in class or on assignments, enables students to restructure their understanding and skills and build more powerful ideas and capabilities. When learners are assessed on what they have learned, their brains must search their memories and retrieve the information. These memory processes help strengthen the learners' knowledge and help maintain that information in an accessible state for later recall. If a person answers incorrectly, the teacher now has a meaningful opportunity to provide feedback, and say, 'A good guess, but that's not quite right . . . this is really the correct answer' or 'Have you considered thinking about the problem this other way . . .?' Search and retrieval practice is often used for:

- self-assessment of knowledge, skills, and attitudes for the purposes of learning
- practice tests and exams.

Formative assessments help make the knowledge gained or not explicit. This can reassure students that they're actually learning or make them clearly aware of areas for development.

You may have identified that formative feedback may be given in replies to students' contributions in class, as well as in written or oral commentary on their work. Some of these views will also form the basis for a summative judgement and the generation of marks and grades. However, part of it will not. If assessment is conceptualised in this way, it is not a bolt on to teaching and learning, but is understood to be an embedded part of the whole process.

Summative assessment

Summative assessment focuses on **learning completed**. It gives learners the opportunity to demonstrate to themselves, to you, to each other or to others who are significant to them:

- how far they have progressed towards the achievement of planned learning outcomes; and
- what other, unexpected advances they have made.

Summative assessment can give a definitive grade and/or make a judgement about the learners' achievement. It can be carried out at particular stages of the course. If the judgement verifies that the learner has met an established standard indicative of special expertise, the judgement may lead to accreditation.

Reaction

When teaching students it is important to ascertain their satisfaction levels. An assessment is used to determine the satisfaction level with learning or assessment experience. These assessments can be carried out at various points in the programme: mid-module, end of module, end of programme through course evaluation sheets. Intrinsic motivation can be linked to feelings of being valued and satisfied with the course and its delivery. As identified by Duckworth et al. (2012: 34):

> Motivation is a key driver in stimulating students and provid-ing an educational experience which offers them the opportu-nity to be productive and have self-respect. It can challenge the inequalities in the learners' lives and provide them with hope and aspirations, which challenge the cycle of poverty and failure. In any area where we intend to inspire motivation, setting both short-term and long-range goals is needed. If the long-term goals clearly contribute to the students' aims in life, they should be more motivating.

Reflection and activity

What questions might you ask to ascertain whether your learners are satisfied and motivated by the course?

You may have considered asking 'Are you enjoying the lessons and the course content?' If the answer is yes, what is it that makes it satisfying and how can you ensure it continues being so? If the answer is no, why isn't it satisfying and how can you change the situation?

In order to ensure that learners are progressing and reaching their potential you may want to build reflective questions into your lessons for both yourself and learners.

Teacher's questions:

1. What do the learners need to know?
2. What do they know?
3. How will I plug the gaps?
4. What is the potential impact?
5. What is the actual impact?

Learner's questions:

1.   What do I need to know?
2.   What do I know?
3.   How will I plug the gaps?
4.   What is the potential impact?
5.   What is the actual impact?

Reflection and activity

Create a feedback strategy you can use with your learners to ascertain their satisfaction with the course. You could use post-it notes, flip charts and colours, words, images etc. What matters is that the learners can express themselves and you can work with them to reflect on the findings and create great lessons.

Effective design of assessment

Alignment of teaching and student learning experiences with syllabus objectives and standards descriptors is achieved through the design of the assessment instrument which is a tool for gathering information about student achievement. An assessment task is a form of assessment instrument that involves learners applying and using relevant knowledge and theoretical and practical skills to create a product or a response to a meaningful problem or issue. It is important to make the objectives explicit to the learners so they are clearly aware that the activities they are engaged in are relevant to their progress which fits with the outcomes. The learning outcomes are statements that predict what learners will gain as a result of learning, so there should be a clear relationship between learning outcomes and assessment. It is possible to assess more than one learning outcome at once as long as all assessment tasks are appropriate to, and in harmony with, the learning outcomes they are meant to assess. Learning outcomes should not be vague and 'woolly'. They should start with a clear statement of what is being assessed and the criteria by which the assessment is being made; these should match the learning goals.

Assessment should be authentic and align with the content of the course. It should fit the learning with the methods matching the type of learning you want to take place. You wouldn't want to check a plumber's practical skill of fitting a washing machine, by asking her/him to write about it.

Reflection and activity

Consider how you implement effective assessment in your subject area.

Read the case study of Health and Social Care Specialist Deborah Parkinson and her approach to effective assessment.

During initial teacher training a placement was obtained at a FE college teaching on a range of programmes within the Childcare department. However, since completing the qualification, experiences within different departments within the college have been gained; this includes teaching two groups of Pre-Access students studying on the Social Sciences pathway at level 2. Both groups include students that have either not accessed education for some time or have had negative experiences in the past. This has proven to be a challenging time where carefully planned sessions have been necessary in order to meet the somewhat negative attitudes of some learners. A humanist approach to teaching and assessment has been adopted in an attempt to build confidence in the learners, based on theory penned by Rogers (1996) who theorised that by looking at the whole person a teacher should build confidence in their learners and encourage their natural curiosity. Similarly, Maslow (1993) supported the humanist approach through his theory of a 'hierarchy of needs' and the motivational growth to self-actualisation based upon intrinsic motivation. With this in mind, assessment of learning using formative strategies throughout each session has ensured that all learners are able to develop not only their confidence but their knowledge and understanding as well as the skills required to meet the criteria for each module. An example of formative assessment is peer assessment, whereby learners are asked to formulate a question for one of their peers to answer; this not only encourages the learners to take ownership of their learning in a student-centred approach, but also as Assessment for Learning (AfL) (Black and William 1998). Hattie (2009: 127) states that 'evaluation and assessment of students provides powerful feedback to teachers about how well they are teaching'. However, Petty (2009: 479) points out that 'assessment results are notoriously poor at predicting future performance'. Granted, but if assessment is valid and in line with the specification of the awarding body, it is making sure that it is the right assessment and is appropriate and applicable. It also needs to be in line with the learning objectives of the session and the activities and learning (Biggs 1999). Assessment also needs to be reliable so that the learners are not being tested unfairly. Petty (2009: 481) states that 'to be truly formative, this information must be used by the learner to improve'. Black and William (1998) point out that learners' grades can be increased through effective formative strategies. However, this form of formative assessment proved to be successful as it not only motivated learners by encouraging them to take ownership of their own learning as well as becoming reflective practitioners, but also endeavoured to inform future planning and assessment strategies. It also enabled the less confident learners, or the learners who may not have understood some of the content of the session, to hear relevant questions and answers being discussed amongst their peers.

Other forms of formative assessment include the use of questions and answers throughout the session aimed at individuals to assess their knowledge and understanding of the concept. The learners have participated in quizzes and word search activities as an informal approach to assessment of learning. Petty (2009: 276) states 'quizzes are always popular; they are enjoyable, arousing and involving – all of which serve to increase their effectiveness'. However, due to a number of learners within the group being easily distracted it was necessary to monitor the groups in an attempt to encourage participation from all by using positive reinforcement (Skinner 1953) through setting targets and goals for success. It was also necessary to prepare a check list to ensure participation from all learners.

Summative assessment on the other hand tends to cause anxiety amongst the students due to their having to work independently to complete a task; for example the learners were asked to produce a leaflet that would address and answer questions relating to the assessment criteria for the module (see Appendix 3). The prepared questions were designed to be scaffolded (Bruner 1985) giving students the chance to reflect upon them and develop concepts in a cognitivist approach before answering. For the more able learners more challenging and thought-provoking questions were included that will enable them to access the higher levels of learning (Bloom 1956). The task proved to meet the needs of all learners, although some learners with Specific Learning Difficulties (SLD) needed additional support. Completion of the summative task will be graded and constructive feedback provided for the students. 'Ideally students use this feedback to derive generic guidance that they then transfer to other academic tasks' (Sambell et al. 2012: 39). This is an area that does need to be developed to ensure that learners are able to reflect upon their prior learning and thus ensure that the assessment has served to develop a deeper knowledge and understanding.

It would appear that there is a need for a varied and flexible approach to teaching and learning activities. It is essential that the learning outcomes are achieved through formative assessment learning activities which are designed to meet the module criteria based around constructive alignment (Biggs 1999). The impact on teaching practice is to be aware of the needs of all learners to ensure that they are involved individually in formative assessment as well as summative assessment to ensure that their needs are met and that they are able to reach their full potential.

When considering assessment it is worth considering **ipsative, norm-referenced** and **criterion-referenced assessment.**

Ipsative assessment is the comparison of a learner's performance in the same domain over time (by a teacher and the learner her/himself). It facilitates students measuring their own progress without comparing it to others. It allows them to set assessment against their 'personal best' performance. For example, in athletics, personal best is an example of ipsative assessment. Ipsative assessment can be both an empowering and motivational tool driven by students taking ownership of and setting their own goals and targets, monitoring their progress and setting future actions. The outcomes can be documented by the student in their individual learning plan which provides a personal account of their educational journey.

Norm-referenced assessment is when the learner achievement is measured relative to the other learners participating in the assessment, for example, other learners in the class.

Criterion-referenced assessment is when the learning progress is measured against defined and objective criteria and standards, for example, the accreditation body.

Reflection and activity

Consider whether you apply **ipsative, norm-referenced and/or criterion-referenced assessment** and the impact on learning and teaching.

Some principles of assessment

Reliability and validity

In order for assessments to be sound, they must be free of bias and distortion. Reliability and validity are two concepts that are important for defining and measuring bias and distortion.

Reliability refers to the extent to which assessments are consistent. Just as we may have reliable household appliances, such as cookers, fridges, washing machines etc., that we expect to work when we need them, we should strive to have reliable, consistent instruments to measure student achievement. Another way to think of reliability is to imagine a kitchen scale. If you weigh 2 kilos of potatoes in the morning, and the scale is reliable, the same scale should register 2 kilos for the potatoes at the end of the day. Similarly, instruments such as classroom assessments should be reliable – it should not make any difference whether a student takes the assessment in the morning or afternoon, one day or the next.

Another measure of reliability is the internal consistency of the items. For example, if you create a quiz to measure students' ability to solve fractions, you should be able to assume that if a student gets an item correct, she or he will also get other, similar items correct.

Validity

Validity refers to how well a test measures what it is supposed to measure. Why is it necessary? While reliability is necessary, it alone is not sufficient. For a test to be reliable, it also needs to be valid. For example, if a surveyor's laser measuring device is not calibrated correctly, then mismeasurements will continually occur, albeit consistently. Thus the reading will be reliable because it consistently reports the same measurement for the same job, but it is not valid because it is not calibrated correctly to give true findings.

Types of validity

These include content, construct, and face.

Content validity means that the test assesses the course content and outcomes using formats familiar to the students.

To understand the traditional definition of **construct validity**, it is first necessary to understand what a construct is. A construct, or psychological construct as it is also called, is an attribute, proficiency, ability, or skill that happens in the human brain and is defined by established theories. For example, 'overall English language proficiency' is a construct. It exists in theory and has been observed to exist in practice.

Face validity means that the test looks as though it measures what it is supposed to measure.

Reflection and activity

Consider ways to improve the validity of your assessments.

You may have noted the following points:

1. Make sure your goals and objectives are clearly defined and operationalised. Expectations of students should be written down.

2. Match your assessment measure to your goals and objectives. Additionally, have the test reviewed by faculty at other schools to obtain feedback from an outside party who is less invested in the instrument.
3. Get students involved; have the students look over the assessment for troublesome wording, or other difficulties.
4. If possible, compare your measure with other measures, or data that may be available.

Reflection and activity

Being a great teacher is about providing equal opportunities for all students and this includes the assessment. Read sociologist and teacher educator, Sue Watmore's case study, in which she provides an example of how a participative formative assessment process led to successful undertaking of a formal summative assessment assignment. Then consider the ways you ensure your assessment strategies provide equality of opportunity.

In this case study I will describe the assessment practice on a module on a full time Access to Teaching Course. The module was focused on supporting learners and is covered over the first semester on a weekly basis. The group was made up of twenty-five learners. The key aim of the module and the way in which it was delivered and assessed was to promote and model best equality practice. My aim in describing this case study is to highlight the issue of equality in assessment and model an example of effective strategies in assessment that promote equality and achievement.

The UK is an unequal society. That inequality is carried over into the education system including the process of learning and assessment. According to the Equality and Human Rights Commission (2010) social class has twice the impact on achievement as ethnicity and five times that of gender. Social class is considered the single biggest factor affecting achievement. Inequality is mediated through the education system.

As Stobart (2005) argues 'students' prior experiences, socio-economic and cultural backgrounds and the educational resources available to them' have a major impact on achievement.

As teachers we need to consider our role; how can we best support our learners in challenging and overcoming inequality and achieving success? Carrying out assessment involves unequal power relations between the institution, the assessor and the learner. It is important to keep in mind that learner experiences of inequality may impact on their sense of self, their self-esteem and confidence.

The way in which learners are assessed may also impact on what they achieve. For example, research has shown that girls are likely to be more successful than boys at open ended writing especially if it includes personal responses. The gap is smaller in multiple choice tests where girls do better on questions relating to the humanities and relationships and boys do better on questions relating to areas such as science, technical matters and sports (Stobart 2005).

Assessments may represent western values and assumptions. A good example of this is IQ tests which Broadfoot (1979 cited in Stobart 2005) argues reflect the cultural values of the test developers. Cook (2000) cited in Stobart (2005) states that the speed element of intelligence tests disadvantages people from cultures who see speed of response with little importance.

Pollitt et al. (2000) cited in Stobart (2005) offer an excellent example of cultural bias in assessment:

'. . . assumptions of mathematics test writers interfered with understanding of an Urdu speaking student taking a mathematics test in English. In Urdu the number of hours "in a day" (din) is 12 (with day-night, dinraath, being 24 hours) and there are 2 words for "height" (from the ground, of the object) – with both ambiguities capable of generating "wrong" answers to everyday "how long would it take . . .?" and "how high is . . . .?" questions.'

The content of assessment is also an issue – whose knowledge and skills are being taught and assessed? Perry and Francis (2010) argue that inclusion of working class people's experience and expertise is a key factor in facilitating their success.

As teachers we have a responsibility to ensure that all learners are equally able to participate and achieve and that we aim for assessment to be as fair as possible. The better we know our learners individually, the better we are able to do this. Building relationships with learners based on mutual trust and respect is essential to designing the most effective assessment strategies.

With a key focus on education as a potentially transformational experience I redesigned the module. My aim was not only to support the learners in demonstrating a deeper understanding of equality and effective equality strategies in the module's summative written assignment; I wanted to raise awareness of patterns of inequality and the impact of this on their learners. I also hoped that through a democratic, participative approach the learners would be able to reflect on and share their own experiences of education. Learners were also encouraged to evaluate the support mechanisms at their placement institutions and critically evaluate their own equality practice. By helping learners to understand the human consequences of inequality I hoped to increase their empathy with their learners and motivate them to take positive action to promote equality in their professional practice. I wanted them to have a passion to support and empower their learners in transforming their lives.

I began by creating the beginnings of an equality handbook outlining the key equality issues in the UK relating to social class, race/ethnicity, gender, sexuality and disability giving an overview then focusing more closely on education. Learners were asked to read sections of the Handbook on a weekly basis to discuss the following week.

I also included some guided readings on research findings on equality in education which class members volunteered to research and present to the group across a number of weeks. This highlighted key research findings relating to different aspects of equality in education. These were discussed and learners were encouraged to make links to their own personal experiences.

Learners also met in small groups to consider the issues presented and to discuss possible strategies that could be adopted both at an individual and institutional level to promote equality.

They were also encouraged to explore how their placement institutions dealt with the issues raised and share this in their small groups. The aim of this was to share and critically develop their ideas on how best to promote equality. The presentations and suggested strategies were recorded weekly on the intranet so that by the end of the module there was a handbook produced by the learners that they could then print off.

Formative assessment was largely informal observation of not just learner presentations but also of the points and reflections raised in discussions as learners developed their critical awareness. Feedback from the learners showed that they particularly valued the participative nature of these discussions especially listening to their peers' experiences of education which personalised the reality of educational inequality and experiences. Giving learners a voice empowered them by valuing their experiences and perspectives.

Collier and Morgan (2007) argue that there is often a gap between lecturers' expectations for assessment tasks and learners' understanding of what is expected of them. This has been shown to particularly impact on disadvantaged groups in higher education. In order to support learners in understanding the requirements of the assessment criteria and unpick the taken for granted and unstated assumptions made by staff, I built in a marking exercise early on in the module. During one session the learners worked in small groups with the assessment criteria to mark and feed back on a past learner's assignment. By discussing the assessment criteria and getting to read a good assignment, learners were able to see a good example of what was expected. Learner feedback showed that this was considered particularly useful and they would have liked other modules to have done this.

Again in order to unpick staff assumptions and learner expectations about the module assessment, one session early on was dedicated to one to one or paired tutorials to discuss the assignment and agree a contract of what the learner would be writing. This helped to clarify any queries and ensure that learners were on the right track.

Throughout the module, learners were encouraged to submit draft answers to each assessment criterion to ensure that they were on the right lines. Each draft received written feedback that was as specific as possible to ensure the learner had clear feedback on what they needed to do to meet the assessment criteria. Where there were issues, either the learner or myself requested a one to one tutorial to discuss feedback and ways forward.

Towards the end of the module learners were requested to submit their drafts so far and another session was dedicated to one to one or paired tutorials in which the written feedback was discussed and ways forward agreed.

Almost all of the learners attended the tutorials and submitted drafts.

In terms of formal assessment, practical teaching observations demonstrated the seriousness with which most learners took in supporting their learners in terms of equality. The summative assessment of the module, the written assignment, showed that the learners' discussions and understanding of equality were greatly improved. Some assignments were very impressive in showing the learners' commitment to and practice in delivering best equality practice. I did not feel that any learners discussed equality in a tokenistic way (which had previously been the case with some learners). No learner failed their assignments on criteria relating to equality. Out of twenty-five learners in the group only two learners did not pass. This was related to problems that they had in starting their placements late on the course.

Communication, feedback and feed-forward

Effective feedback is vital to excellent teaching and learning. One way of increasing the effectiveness of feedback and the likelihood that the information provided is understood is to conceptualise feedback more as a *dialogue* rather than as information transmission. Feedback as dialogue means that the student not only receives feedback information but also has the opportunity to engage with the discussion about that feedback. It is vital that it is a two-way process where the students' views, feelings, hopes etc. are valued, listened to and acted upon. Students value feedback, especially when given by someone whom they respect for their knowledge, attitude, fairness and authenticity. Failing to give feedback is in itself a non-verbal communication, which may lead the student to feel devalued and demotivated.

Two-way verbal communication can also be used to build and sustain strong and rewarding relationships with your students that are based on learning from each other and together creating meaningful knowledge.

Students need *specific* and *timely* feedback on their work. If feedback is given too late, it may no longer seem relevant to the student. Therefore, feedback should not be left until the end of a unit/module, as the student is unlikely to benefit from it once the task is complete and they have moved on to a new one. However, providing feedback too soon may disturb the student's reflective process. An essential function of assessment is helping students to learn and part of this process is reflection. Great quality, comprehensive, timely feedback is a very important factor in driving student learning forward.

Reflection and activity

What does effective feedback look like in your classroom?

Feedback should not be just about giving students a grade. A grade or mark tells students something about the effectiveness of their learning, but not very much. Feedback should enable students to realise where they have done well and indicate what they could improve on, as well as justifying the grade/mark of summative assessments.

Generic statements about the general quality of analysis may be of little use. Really thorough marking involves pointing out each individual's strengths and areas for development. A guiding principle is that students should get feedback on one piece of work in time for this to be of benefit for the next. A useful strategy for overwhelmed markers (which I for one have experienced!) is to comment intensively on one section of a piece of work, as an example of how the student should go about addressing any areas for development.

Don't over assess learners

A very substantial assessment load does not allow students time to comprehend and explore material; it tends to push them into shallow, rote approaches to learning, where they try to find quick solutions and formulae for tasks, without really understanding central principles. If students are confronted with too many assessments, particularly if this involves a repetitive approach, they are also likely to get bored, lose attentiveness and motivation.

The benefits of successful feedback set in the context of learning outcomes are many. For example, successful feedback will:

- build confidence in the learners
- motivate learners to improve their learning
- provide learners with performance improvement information

- correct errors
- identify strengths and areas for development.

Final thoughts

The more organised you are as the teacher the easier it will be for others to learn from you. It's critical, therefore, to understand how people learn, what they have in fact learned, and whether this knowledge is useful for their particular chosen path. That's why the foundation of developing successful course materials is the effective use of assessments. Assessment is an integral part of the learning process, and will be formative and diagnostic as well as summative and evaluative, providing feedback to students wherever appropriate. The feedback given should support and empower the student to take informed action and responsibility for their future learning and development.

Further reading

Perry, E. and Francis, B. (2010) *The Social Class Gap for Educational Achievement: A Review of the Literature*. RSA Projects available at www.thersa.org/-data/assets/pdf_file/0019/367003/RSA-Social-Justice-paper.pdf

Stobart, G. (2005) 'Fairness in multicultural assessment systems.' *Assessment in Education: Principles, Policy and Practice,* 12: 3, 275–287.

Powell, S. and Tummons, J. (2012) *Inclusive Practice in the Lifelong Learning Sector*. Exeter: Learning Matters.

Websites

Equality and Human Rights Commission. *How Fair is Britain?:* www.equalityhumanrights.com

The National Institute of Adult Continuing Education (Niace): http://www.niace.org.uk/

Talent (training adult literacy, ESOL and numeracy teachers): http://www.talent.ac.uk/

Chapter 8

How will I know if it's working?

Chapter objectives

This chapter provides an insight into evaluating your own practice and learner feedback on your sessions. It also considers reflecting on your practice to make it better and quality assurance in teaching.

What is evaluation?

If assessment is about identifying the changes which have taken place in the learners, i.e. measuring learning, then the word 'evaluation' is generally reserved for a broader approach to asking how successful the teaching and learning process was. Broadly, if we assess student learning, then we evaluate sessions or courses or whole curricula. Are we doing what we set out to do? Are we achieving the purposes of the lesson or the programme or the college? This process is obviously tied into the growing need for professionals and their institutions to be accountable to others, whether this is the increasing numbers of inspectors from outside bodies, the industry for which we are preparing people or the local community we aim to serve.

Key concepts for evaluation

Assessment – means making a judgement about whether learners have learned what we intended them to learn, e.g. by a test or exam.

Evaluation – means making a judgement about whether or not the educational process (e.g. lesson, programme, college) has achieved what it set out to do, e.g. by an end of course questionnaire.

Validation – is a process whereby a body (usually an outside group like an exam board or a professional association) makes a judgement on whether a programme should be authorised to start or continue (e.g. can this college teach a particular BTEC programme).

Appraisal – is an organisational process whereby a college or centre makes judgements about the professional performance of a member of staff as measured against targets or performance indicators.

Why evaluate?

Sometimes teachers ask why it is necessary to evaluate their sessions or programmes. Surely, it is sometimes argued, the assessment process itself is sufficient. If students pass their exams or complete their projects or (perhaps most often cited) get jobs – then we must be doing OK and other kinds of measures are not needed.

This is an interesting view because of course all three of these things – qualifications, student achievement and employment are vitally important in answering the question of how well we are doing. However there is no single measure that tells us that a programme or a session is a good one. Sometimes students can pass exams after boring and unchallenging programmes and it might be that they were recruited to a course that was beneath their ideal level. Equally it is possible to have courses which are rich and fulfilling and of huge value but where students do not (all) achieve the target they aimed at.

It can even be that in some cases students get jobs in spite of their training not because of it and have to 're-learn' the essential skills and knowledge when they are out in practice.

Clearly there are broader questions to ask about how good a programme or a particular approach to teaching is.

It is also worth approaching this question from an individual professional perspective. One aspect of professionalism we discussed earlier is the idea of the professional as a reflective practitioner (see Chapter 1). In this sense part of being professional is the need to constantly review and evaluate your own practice. Am I teaching in the best way for these learners? Did this session achieve its aims? Am I meeting the needs of all the different learners – engaging the less committed students and challenging the ones who perhaps find this material straightforward?

There is a sense (strongly advocated by John Elliott, 2007) in which teachers can be seen as only truly professional when they are researching into their own practice. This is a kind of ad hoc 'seat of the pants' action research where every innovation or change in practice is seen as a small scale inquiry project and the aim is to refine techniques, methods and resources so as to best meet learners' needs.

There is also a broader issue of accountability. Of course in recent years most professionals in education have been bombarded with different attempts to 'call them to account'. Many feel 'inspected to death' and there is a strong argument that this approach has undermined teachers' sense of professional autonomy and independence. Nevertheless it is not appropriate to respond to this 'culture of accountability' by asking simply to be left alone and trusted.

Further Education is an expensive process. In most towns the most costly piece of capital equipment apart from the hospital is the FE College and these are often accompanied by adult centres and outreach units which add to the expense. In the private sector, training and staff development make up a significant part of the budget of many companies. It is reasonable for the members of the community who pay for this service to ask that it is run effectively and professionally and to be interested in the arguments teachers give for the choices they make about methods and resources.

So an additional element of the professional task is the requirement to explain – to defend and argue for the job that we do and the way that we do it. Evaluation (does it do what it says on the tin?) is an essential part of this.

What should be evaluated?

Nearly all teachers have an approach which involves a great deal of informal almost 'invisible' evaluation as their sessions go on. Did that last explanation make sense? Is the diagram clear? Did you find the group work interesting? This is often tied up with the kind of informal assessment feedback we discussed earlier. For example, what are the implications of all this for starting a new business? What are the four key safety issues to be considered before work starts? Identify the problems of a declining tourist destination.

These help the teacher answer the question of whether the learning has taken place (assessment) but they also cast light on the question of whether the session is going well (evaluation).

At the same time there are a range of other informal signals which tell the teacher how things are going. All teachers come to recognise the 'buzz' of true engagement, for example, when students are working in groups, and are able to distinguish it from the 'racket' of discussions of what happened at the weekend or what was on telly last night.

Teachers also use semi-formal techniques like 'talking walls' and stop-start-continue exercises to gain some 'quick and dirty' feedback from students without taking up large amounts of teaching/learning time.

Talking walls are spaces where learners can record their thoughts and feelings in relation to a number of different topics. Noticeboards/whiteboards are located around the walls of a room which learners can use to reflect on the issues and respond with comments. The walls can be paper or whiteboards or learners can use post-it notes which can be stuck on to a surface. The talking wall can be used as part of a brief activity or left up for a longer period of time to produce more feedback. The activity can take place physically or virtually using a discussion board, blog page or wiki.

The process includes the following elements:

- Learners are asked to reflect on the statements/questions and think about what they mean to them.
- When they are ready, learners approach the talking wall and write their answer/response to the statements/questions.
- At the end of the process, the material generated is shared with the learners. If the wall is used by a number of groups it is a good idea to take a photo of the wall and the feedback, for example, the post-it notes.
- Where possible, points that have been raised are addressed in an open forum to demonstrate commitment to making changes/learning from learner feedback in a transparent and democratic way.

The Stop/Start/Continue activity is used for a variety of purposes related to development and communication, team-building and troubleshooting. This technique is great for generating respectful, honest and meaningful communication. At the end of a teaching session ask learners to write the following on a post-it note:

1. List one or two things I'm currently doing that are not working (I should **STOP** doing them).
2. List one or two things that would be beneficial for me to **START** doing.
3. List one or two things I am currently doing that I should **CONTINUE**.

Other strategies for collecting feedback include a **suggestion box.** This can also be used as strategy to improve your teaching by helping you identify new topics, instructional strategies, activities, and assignments that may better meet your learners' needs.

To use the suggestion box technique, bring a small box (maybe a shoe box) or a large envelope to each class session or hang an envelope on your office door. Invite students to provide feedback that focuses on areas of your teaching they would like to see you modify, classroom activities or assignments they might find useful, and topics about which they would like to learn more. When learners focus on an area of improvement in your teaching, instruct them to identify not only the weak areas or deficiencies but also how you could improve your teaching in those areas.

An advantage of the suggestion box is that students may feel more comfortable critiquing you and providing constructive feedback because their comments are anonymous. Another advantage is that it does not detract from teaching to implement. Learners can put suggestions in the box as they are leaving the classroom or before they start. Promptly review students' suggestions, summarise suggestions for your class, and make adjustments to your teaching as soon as possible or indicate why you will not make the suggested change.

Where there is time you could also hand round **brief evaluation sheets** at the end of a session. This is especially important where teachers are innovating or trying out different approaches and can help to decide on the value of a particular change.

Evaluation

Increasingly evaluation is a more formal process whereby students fill in prepared questionnaires, usually at key points during or after a module or programme. These materials feed into a quality assurance process within the institution, and are sometimes carried out independently of the teacher.

Here it is worth examining the questions that are asked as they often indicate the organisational priorities of the college or centre and may not necessarily pick up on the particular aims of the course. An obvious example may be 'difficult' though necessary modules like business numeracy or caterers' French. Students may find these sessions less 'fun' than other courses, but given time will acknowledge their importance. A simple tick-box evaluation on one day might well produce a much more short-term negative view.

Who evaluates?

This may seem a question with an obvious answer – it's the teacher's job surely, but it raises the wider question of whose experience and whose opinions are taken into account when evaluation happens. A useful idea is to think of the different people involved in a learning process as 'stakeholders'. A stakeholder is anyone who has an interest in a process, so it obviously includes teachers and students as well as managers and officers of the college or centre. They are affected by the success or failure of the programmes or sessions. However it is possible to draw larger and larger circles and identify stakeholders outside the institution – employers and colleagues of the students we hope to educate, for example. This is clearest on day-release or other sponsored programmes where there may be mechanisms for reporting directly to current or future employers. In the case of young students or those with learning difficulties it may well be thought appropriate to ask for the views of parents or carers.

It is also worth remembering what we mentioned earlier about the college or adult centre as a community resource – there is a sense here that everyone is a stakeholder in education as we all live alongside the people who are trained or educated. In the case of vocational education we all have an interest in living in a society with well educated and skilful plumbers, hairdressers, gardeners and chefs, while adult learning has long been associated with projects to develop and empower communities on a local or regional basis.

Obviously some of these stakeholder groups are easier to consult than others and it can be difficult to ensure representative views when trying to identify the attitude of the industry or the community, but when whole programmes or curricula are being evaluated this can be a worthwhile thing to do. Broadly speaking the more different 'voices' you can include in an evaluation the more likely you are to have a full picture. This process whereby a range of different viewpoints are sought is often referred to as 'triangulation', a word which derives from navigation at sea where the more different direction signals a boat receives the more accurately it will be possible to get an exact location. Similarly with education, if we can plot 'lines' from students and teachers and managers and employers and the local community, then we are likely to obtain a fuller picture of whether we are achieving our aims.

Reflection and activity

Who are the stakeholders in your organisation?
What impact do they have on the evaluation process?

What kind of questions do we ask when we evaluate?

One obvious response to this is to look at the aims and objectives of the session or programme. If the point of the programme is properly expressed in its 'intended learning outcomes', then it seems clear that the overriding concern of evaluation would be to determine whether or not these outcomes have been achieved.

Did the students pass their exams or tests? Did they complete their projects or hand in their lab records? Did they demonstrate the skills which the course was trying to teach them? One step further would be to ask if they got the jobs they were looking for or returned to their workplaces as better practitioners.

These are all of course valid and vital questions. There is little point in setting out a series of objectives for a learning programme if you then fail to record the extent to which they were achieved. This approach is sometimes referred to as **summative evaluation.** It involves drawing up a kind of balance sheet of end results. Its effectiveness depends on the way in which data is collected and how it is interpreted. Exam results are not a *direct* indicator of how good a programme was, for example.

Poorer results could reflect a tougher exam or a weaker original cohort of students while the learning experience remained the same. Similarly, a strongly motivated, resourceful group of learners can sometimes overcome the consequences of bad teaching and achieve well despite the way they were prepared rather than because of it. Whether or not students go on to get jobs is likely to be affected by labour market conditions which have little to do with how well they were trained.

It is also worth asking about time scale. Most education programmes claim to be 'in it for the long haul'. Their aim is to produce practitioners or citizens who will use the skills and knowledge and live by the values which the course imparts throughout their career, yet evaluation processes often stop tracking students after a year or so. Every teacher will have encountered students who they meet again long after the course to be told, 'I didn't realise how valuable that stuff you taught us was going to be until years later'.

The key problem with summative evaluation though is that it focuses on outcomes without really looking at the programme itself. After all if we are interested in the quality of a process we go through we are probably going to ask questions about what it was like to be involved – the 'how was it for you?' question.

The approach which stresses the educational experience is sometimes called illuminative evaluation. This is because it asks questions in an attempt to 'throw light' on what the course was like. How interesting was it to be on? How actively did the learners engage with the materials? Did people feel challenged? Did they enjoy the experience?

By and large this approach reflects the common sense view of what evaluation is about. As teachers, we tend not to go home at the end of the day feeling good or bad about our work on the basis of assessment of objectives or measurement of outcomes. What makes us feel good about sessions is the sense of a 'buzz' – that students enjoyed what they did, were engaged and challenged and interacted with the subject and each other. These are all 'process' issues of the kind we discussed in an earlier chapter – they are about what actually happens rather than outcomes which are the 'product' of the session.

These process issues can often be more difficult to identify and measure in ways that make sense to outsiders. It is easier to find out how far a student can jump after a sports coaching session on long jump (and compare it to where they started from) than it is to assess how far they worked effectively with their coach, got on with other jumpers, felt involved in the conduct of the session or simply enjoyed themselves.

It can easily seem that illuminative evaluation in its enthusiasm for experience and giving the full picture can miss out on what made people come along in the first place – jumping further!

For this reason evaluation of outcomes – summative evaluation – tends to be more popular with people who are paying for programmes (especially sponsoring others) than illuminative evaluations which 'tell the story' of the educational experience.

Illuminative approaches, however, because they focus on the processes and experiences within the course can often pick up unintended outcomes – all those things students learn which are impossible to identify in advance and these can often be the intangible but vital aspects of their learning (self-confidence, self-esteem, ability to work together, acceptance of others etc.) which have the greatest long-term impact on learners.

What should happen to the information we collect?

It is important to stress that collecting information from different sources, asking the class, listing test results, sending questionnaires to employers or ex-students etc. is only the first part of an evaluation process. In an area like education nothing could be more misleading than the old saying 'The facts speak for themselves'. In the case of evaluation data this is clearly not true – satisfaction scores or exam grades are absolutely vital but they have to be interpreted. They need to be set in the context of the overall aims of the institution and the curriculum, the nature of the student body, etc.

Only after this process has happened can decisions be taken about changing programmes, altering methods, employing new resources, tightening admissions procedures, etc. Going straight from data to decisions is like a patient taking his own temperature and then going for an ice bath to bring it down without considering causes and context. Part of being a professional is the ability to weigh different pieces of information and make appropriate choices in a critically reflective way.

At the same time of course it is important that evaluation feedback is acted upon. We have probably all been in situations where we have been asked for our opinions and felt reluctant to participate because we did not feel that it had any effect. It is important to make sure that feedback is taken into account when decisions are made and that this is communicated to the students, staff and other stakeholders who took part.

Reflecting on your teaching

We all reflect on, or informally think about, pedagogical experiences we have during a day. You can think about your teaching before, during, and after a lesson. No single time is right in every circumstance. Reflective teaching means looking at what you do in the classroom, thinking about why you do it, and thinking about whether it works. This is a process of self-observation and self-evaluation. By collecting information about what goes on in our classroom, and by analysing and evaluating this information, we can clearly identify and explore our own practices, assumptions, beliefs and values.

You may think about what you are doing and how effective you are, even if you are not conscious of the fact. Monitor the level of understanding, check that the resources are at the correct level, and make judgements about the engagement of your classes. As you do this you may make adjustments immediately. This may then lead to changes and improvements in your teaching.

Further questions you may begin to ask yourself to begin the reflective process include:

- How do I interact with learners?
- How do I respond when they ask questions?
- What kind of classroom atmosphere do I create?
- What kinds of questions do I ask?
- Is my classroom spontaneous or is it predictable?
- Are my learners involved?
- Why didn't a session go well?
- Why did a session go well?

Reflection and activity

Set aside some time soon after your next teaching session to address the points above. It may be helpful to keep a diary to record your reflection and refer to this in future. It's also a good idea to take into account the opinions of others. For example, you could encourage colleagues/peers to offer observations on your performance. Feedback from learners can also offer an important indication of your effectiveness.

Below Samantha Watter's shares her views on reflection.

Reflection is a very personal process and involves looking at my experiences in my teaching sessions and adapting my practices and strategies to provide the best experiences for my particular learners. I have included entries that reflect on behaviour, assessment and feedback to learners, individual target setting, inclusivity/access and my specialist area. Many of my reflections incorporate several of these in one session and by reviewing these and adding to them at a later date, I believe my teaching skills, professional skills and personal attributes have grown and developed in the past year and I have grown as a person and a teacher. My knowledge, skills and practices have been driven by the reflective process. I have become more confident and organised.

Trainee teacher and hairdressing specialist, Hannah Ratcliffe, suggests reflection strategies:

- Keep a journal of each class or lecture. Before the session, record your learning objectives, planned activities and approaches. Afterwards, assess whether these were successful and/or appropriate. What might you do differently next time?
- Record your classes (audio and/or video) in order to gain the audience's perspective of your performance. Review your delivery style, speech, non-verbal communication and movement around the room.

How can students be involved in reflection?

Though reflection is an important process for teachers and student teachers, it should also be encouraged for the students. Just as teachers grow and develop, so do students and they can only benefit from noticing their development. Many teachers do not know, however, how best to involve students in the process of reflection. Here are some suggestions:

- Give the students opportunities to reflect in different ways, whether it be in writing or out loud. Different materials can also be used to facilitate reflection and keep the students engaged; some students enjoy journaling, some might prefer interviews, and some might prefer blogging. Don't be afraid to use technology, such as blogs and on-line forums.

- Give the students support and direction for their reflection. Simply asking them to reflect will not be enough for all students; guiding questions or introductory sentences can be used to direct the students who need the direction (e.g. Today what I liked was . . . or What did you like today? What helped me learn was . . . or What helped you learn today?).

- Make reflection happen regularly. The more the students take part in reflection, the easier and more natural it will become for them.

- Keep the students' reflections in a portfolio; this way the students will be able to look back on their own reflections to see how much they've grown, learned, and how much they were able to write about their learning.

- Let the students know why they are reflecting – give it purpose and meaning. These reflections help you improve as a teacher, and help them improve as learners; once students know how they learn best, then learning will become easier.

Quality and quality assurance

Quality assurance is the systematic evaluation of the service that you provide and it should be undertaken in a reflective manner as discussed above (and in Chapter 1). As identified in your institutions' approach, quality assurance is largely based on the teaching and learning process, and quite rightly as our learners are at the centre of our service, it is important to begin with them. Rogers (2002) talks about the importance of the evaluation of education:

> To improve our performance as teachers. Questions of quality, of accountability, of protecting our 'customers', of being effective, are important not just for the providers and organisers but also for our student participants and for ourselves.
>
> (Rogers 2002: 255)

Quality assurance helps to support teachers and build expertise and capacity in the education system to deliver positive outcomes for young people and adults. Through sharing, understanding and applying standards and expectations, quality assurance helps to raise standards and expectations, and levels of consistency across teachers, schools, colleges and training providers.

Ofsted is the Office for Standards in Education, Children's Services and Skills. Ofsted inspects schools, colleges, initial teacher education, work-based learning and skills training, adult and community learning, education and training in prisons and other secure establishments, and the Children and Family Court Advisory Support Service (Cafcass). Ofsted also assesses children's services in local areas, and inspects services for looked after children and child protection. Ofsted will only consider a provider to be outstanding for overall effectiveness if they have outstanding teaching, learning and assessment.

You may have identified that Ofsted:

- utilise a range of feedback opportunities for learners, partners and staff so that they can evaluate the service they provide;
- systematically observe and evaluate teaching and learning;
- through performance management and management information systems enable effective data analysis and target setting;
- benchmark our performance and standards through comparison with other adult and community learning provision;
- work to a learner charter that sets out the minimum standards that learners are entitled to receive, supported by an easily accessible and responsive complaints procedure;
- share best practice across the area so that all learners benefit from consistently high standards;
- establish working and steering groups to evaluate and improve specific aspects of performance;

- assess strengths and areas for development and produce an annual self-assessment report (SAR);
- write a quality improvement plan that focuses upon building and maintaining strengths and addressing areas for development;
- develop written policies and procedures to support all staff and learners;
- implement staff development to encourage the sharing of good practice, which includes promoting equality of opportunity and diversity.

Behaviour and quality assurance

Behaviour is increasingly becoming an area for scrutiny and the new Ofsted framework for school inspection (Ofsted 2012a) makes this clear. The four key inspection headings are:

- quality of teaching
- the quality of leadership and management
- the behaviour and safety of pupils
- the achievement of pupils.

Inspectors are asked to make a judgement about students' behaviour in the classroom, especially that of persistent low level disruptive behaviour, and over time through evaluation of sanction and rewards, fixed term and permanent exclusions, or repeated incidences of bullying (the issue is not the number of recorded incidents but the action taken and how effective the action has been (Ofsted 2012a Subsidiary Guidance No. 110166)).

As identified by Duckworth et al. (2012), behaviour is not so easily measured or evaluated in Further Education (FE) and training provider settings where many students who are disaffected can choose to vote with their feet. This can see students choosing not to attend lessons or when they do attend arriving late or/and leaving early. This can be demoralising for the teacher as well as disrupting other students in the class. Proposed changes to the way in which these organisations are to be inspected have been published as part of a consultation on the changes to the Common Inspection Framework implemented in September 2012. The Common Inspection Framework is used in the inspection of all providers who deliver education and training to those aged 16 or over, with the exception of sixth forms and Higher Education (HE); this includes work-based learning providers, Adult and Community Learning, Offender Learning and Next Step Provision as well as colleges of FE. The new proposals have taken into account the changes in legislation and policy as reflected in the Education Act 2011 and significant White Papers such as the schools White Paper, *The Importance of Teaching* (2010).

The consultation proposes three headline grades:

- outcomes for students
- the quality of teaching, learning and assessment
- leadership and management.

It also makes clear the need to evaluate the effectiveness of learner outcomes:

> We propose to judge outcomes for students by giving particular attention to how well:
>
> - All students achieve
> - Gaps are narrowing between different groups of students
> - Students develop personal social and employability skills
> - Students progress to higher level qualifications, and into jobs that meet local and national needs.
>
> (Ofsted 2012a)

Behaviour will be evaluated as part of equality and diversity through 'teaching, learning and assessment, and the behaviour and attitudes of students and staff' (Ofsted 2012b: 10). Many training providers have been used to providing employability skills and functional skills, often accessing funding which specifically focuses on groups such as those young people who are Not in Education, Employment or Training (NEETS). Whilst FE has traditionally been a place of choice, and in particular seen to offer 'second chances' and vocational pathways, changes in culture and policy have led to forced participation for students who may, in previous generations, have been able to access viable employment alternatives to education or training at the age of 16 and 17. A lack of viable choices and progression can lead to disaffection and unwanted behaviour as a reflection of these structural changes. Duckworth et al. (2012)

propose a move from a deficit model of behaviour management which positions the learner as lacking, and instead move towards a more holistic solutions-based approach.

Reflection and activity

> Learners, who have diminished self-esteem and resilience, can struggle to reach their potential both in and out of the classroom. The reasons for this are varied and complex and their difficulties can be compounded by the responses they elicit in others. By building positive and democratic attachments with learners, the more vulnerable, who have perhaps previously had negative experiences of education, can begin to re-experience more positive and hopeful relationships, greater emotional wellbeing and begin to engage more successfully and positively in learning.
>
> Consider the strategies you can put in place to establish a positive and nourishing learning environment.

You may have considered the following:

- Increase your knowledge and experience interacting with learners.
- Know and demonstrate knowledge about individual students' backgrounds, interests, emotional strengths and academic levels.
- Express warm, positive and enthusiastic responses as you interact with students. Show them you care and that you too are passionate about your subject and learning!
- Be attentive to your students' learning needs.
- Show your pleasure and enjoyment of students.
- Interact in a responsive and respectful manner.

This recognises a main drive of the education system in a democratic society is to offer quality education for *all* students so that they can reach their *full* potential and contribute to and participate in that society throughout their lives.

Codes of practice

Part of a teacher's role is also to adhere to the relevant codes of practice and regulatory requirements that surround the profession. There is also a set of legislative Acts that need to be adhered to, which includes, for example, the Health and Safety at Work Act 1974, the Data Protection Act 2010, and the Equality Act 2010.

The teacher's role embodies social justice and promotes equality. It is the responsibility of the teacher to value diversity amongst their students. At a national level this might refer to promoting a greater social equality by providing people with the skills to find work and sustain employment, which may provide greater chances for social mobility (Field 2010).

Reflection and activity

An institutional quality assurance strategy generally aims to improve the effectiveness and efficiency of the educational provision they offer and to make sure that it meets the needs of our learners.

How does the institution where you are based do the above?

Final thoughts

Within the education and training environment, QA is tending towards an almost exclusively results-and-inspection-driven model. QA systems have an unfortunate habit of becoming bureaucratic and clumsy – with each recognition of a supposed weakness resulting in additional measures being added into the system. The resultant proliferation of paperwork is likely to make QA *less* rather than *more* effective. It could be argued that the most effective QA is born of professionalism. It is, in effect, more about maintaining your passion and commitment than a proliferation of paperwork. As a teacher you will work across faculties and disciplines to meet the diverse needs of your learners. Teachers are the most important resource that a student can encounter. They can influence whether learning is a positive or not so positive experience for the student. Part of the drive to ensure learners have positive experiences can be located in the push towards raising the standards of teaching and placing the learner at the heart of the learning and teaching process.

Further reading

Hattie, J. (2011) *Visible Learning for Teachers: Maximising Impact on Learning*. London: Routledge.
Hayes, D., Marshall, T. and Turner, A. (2007) *A Lecturer's Guide to Further Education*. Maidenhead: Open University.
Huddleston, P. and Unwin, L. (2013) *Teaching and Learning in Further Education: Diversity and Change*. London: Routledge.

Websites

National Research and Development Centre (NRDC): http://www.nrdc. org.uk/publications.asp
Ofsted: Common Inspection Framework 2012: http://www.ofsted.gov.uk/ resources/common-inspection-framework-2012
The Quality Assurance Agency (QAA): http://www.qaa.ac.uk/Assuring StandardsAndQuality/quality-code/Pages/default.aspx

Chapter 9

Learning to Learn

Chapter objectives

This chapter provides an overview of being a professional in the Lifelong Learning Sector and considers working in 'learning' organisations. To support this it examines balancing home life, study and teaching and being a lifelong learner yourself. I also explore treating each other as professionals, working in teams, departments and institutions and dealing with policy, research and initiatives.

Introduction

Some of you may have gained skills, experience and knowledge through another trade or profession, for example, as a chef, hairdresser or bricklayer. Whatever your trajectory into teaching you will share the common purpose of meeting the needs of your learners, community and employers.

Reflection and activity

Consider your own journey into teaching and what being a professional means to you.

Read Stephen Jepson-Swallow's journey into teaching and his experience of becoming a great teacher.

I trained at Tameside College of Technology between 1988 and 1990 to become a professional chef. I have had a wide variety of jobs in the catering industry, where I have gained immense experience in the field. Starting off at Manchester Airport for Select Service Partner Restaurants from 1990 to 1999, I worked in both kitchen and front of house from chef de partie to sous chef and assistant manager. I left the airport to join Manchester United as sous chef. I was promoted to head chef after 12 months where I was involved in training chefs with Heathcoat's trainers; my last trainee became my sous chef and is now executive chef at Twickenham Stadium. I left United to open a new RBS-Hardman boulevard, Manchester. I then had two years in contract catering for a variety of companies. In 2007 I was employed by Ribby Hall Village as executive chef, where I was to oversee two restaurants, one café and a busy conference and banqueting centre. Training has always been important to me. I have always enjoyed transferring my skills and knowledge to colleagues. Due to the senior positions I have held and responsibility for training staff, I have always had ambition to be involved in education. I felt I had so much to offer young people wanting to make a career as a chef. Having reached a point in my career, I felt the time had come to share my knowledge and enthuse the chefs of the future. In October 2010, I was given the chance to become a chef lecturer at Hopwood Hall College, where I teach a wide variety of sessions and learners. I have undertaken my NVQ level 3 in Professional cookery, A1 assessors' award and I'm currently studying at Edge Hill University, Certificate of Higher Education in PGCE. This is the most fulfilling and enjoyable job I have had; there is no feeling like seeing students overcoming their own limitations and obstacles to prepare some amazing dishes. I believe it's very important to have subject-specialist teachers with a great practical knowledge base as well as being able to provide excellent theoretical sessions. In the three years I have been employed as a lecturer, I have updated my knowledge by continuous professional development (CPD), including training and work experience and pride myself on training students to leave work ready, with *en trend* skills, ideas and techniques. I also make links from the classroom to real world environment and regularly put lesson scenarios into real incidents from my catering career. These are key elements for me and I believe that my experience and the way I teach modern methods of preparation and cookery, for example, sous vide and molecular gastronomy, goes some way to making me an outstanding teacher. In my last teaching observation this was confirmed by gaining a grade 1 against Ofsted criteria.

These are aspects that make an outstanding teacher:

- embedding language (meta-language) and functional skills – classical French catering terminology
- quality of teaching, learning and assessment – learners benefit from high expectations, engagement, care, support and motivation from staff
- creativity and initiative – students benefit from opportunities to be creative, to express their imagination and to stimulate their senses by coming up with their own final dishes
- linking theory to practice – by having strong subject specialism
- employability skills – to prepare students to work in the industry.

'Learning' organisations

The emergence of the idea of the 'learning organisation' is wrapped up with notions such as 'the learning society'. A learning organisation may be defined as an organisation that learns and encourages learning among its people. It promotes exchange of information between employees, hence creating a more knowledgeable and meaningful workforce. This produces a very flexible organisation where people will accept and adapt to new ideas and changes through a shared vision. According to Senge (1990, p. 3), a learning organisation is one where:

> people continually expand their capacity to create the results they truly desire, where new and expansive patterns of thinking are nurtured, where collective aspiration is set free, and where people are continually learning how to learn together.

If we look at organisations that are acknowledged exemplars for the training and development of their workforces, we can identify the key characteristics that seem to identify such an organisation. These characteristics include:

- valuing individual and organisational learning as a prime means of delivering the organisational mission;
- involving all its members through continuous reflection in a process of continual review and improvement;
- structuring work in such a way that work tasks are used as opportunities for continuous learning.

Reflection and activity

Consider whether your institution seems unmotivated or uninterested in providing a 'learning' organisation for the workforce.

Communication and team collaboration

No wo/man is an island. Two heads are better than one. A problem shared is a problem solved – these are just some of the proverbs that tell of the virtues of teamwork, but when speaking to teachers a number feel isolated from colleagues and peers. A community of sharing among teachers allows them to feel supported by other teachers in their drive to better serve the needs of their students. Effective teams are characterised by trust, respect, and honesty; teachers feel comfortable acknowledging what they do not know without feeling embarrassed or vulnerable because it is assumed that everyone in the group faces challenges and also has knowledge to offer the group. Communication, honesty, and openness allow each individual in the group to contribute to the wealth of knowledge that is shared by the group. Collaboration can be a very empowering tool. It can nurture and ignite enthusiasm and creativity among individuals, teams and organisations.

Reflection and activity

Consider the benefits of collaboration and how you can further your own collaborations.

You may have identified that collaborations can:

- build trust and create relationships
- share a goal
- share accountability
- be open to other team members' ideas.

Good communication and team work

In working to meet the needs of your learners it is vital that you communicate effectively and work well within your team, across the college or institution and where appropriate within a multi-disciplinary partnership. Many of you will bring current and innovative skills which you can share with other trainees and qualified tutors. For example, if you are teaching childcare you may be fresh from working in a nursery and be up-to-date with the latest policies and practice. Sharing your knowledge and skills can be very rewarding. However, for others it may also be frustrating if you feel the skills are not being recognised or realised. For example, if you have been a manager in your previous employment and held a great deal of responsibility and status, not having the same autonomy as a trainee or newly qualified teacher can prove to be a steep learning curve. You may encounter incidences you once had the power to change but cannot because you are now the most junior member of the team. The key is to remember you are now on another track and need to develop your knowledge in this new area. The skills you have are transferrable, and the opportunity to use them will come at different stages of your career.

Below trainee teacher and history specialist Mike Bailey explores the importance of effective teamwork in maintaining a professional approach to teaching in the Lifelong Learning Sector.

An issue which should not be underestimated in importance with regard to Continued Professional Development (CPD) is the need to enhance one's own interpersonal skills and ability to work well as part of a team within an educational institution for the greater good. Teachers who find themselves working together in a college, specifically within the same department, often find that they share the same common professional goals and vested interest, first and foremost in the learners. The craft of teaching is at times ambiguous, yet perhaps an accurate evaluation of the vocation is that it relies more than anything else on effective problem solving; problem solving is a skill we acquire from an early age when we are met with simple mathematical problems, yet within the field of teaching effective problem solving centres around the issue of how we can deliver the very best in teaching in order to obtain the best from our learners in the classroom. This is why teamwork in the workplace is the key ingredient to success in any teaching environment.

Every school and college will have an organisational structure of different staff with different job roles on their payroll. Indeed, with regard to the composite of an organisation's staffing, it will not be uncommon to encounter the following positions (Knight 1997):

• the board of governors (including chairperson, staff governors, parent governors, student governors and local authority-appointed governors)
• the Head/Principal (responsible for the executive operations of the organisation)
• senior management team (often comprising the offices of Head, Deputy, Director of Learner Services)
• middle management (Curriculum Heads, Assistant Curriculum Heads, Coordinators and Directors of departments).
• support staff (specialist workers employed to offer additional specialist care to learners where appropriate)
• personal tutors and mentors (teaching staff appointed as a responsible point of contact to a group of learners)
• subject-specific teachers and teaching assistants (with responsibilities to their own department)
• administrative staff.

It is worth noting that teaching environments are often as diverse a place concerning staff with different skills and training, as they are in learners with different abilities, ethnicities, etc. The wide set of skills available in a school and college should be recognised and capitalised upon by all members of staff through teamwork, with different specialist input being called upon wherever necessary. For example, if we are to consider the chief aim of all members of staff in a school or college to be the safeguarding of the learners and a duty to provide them with pastoral care and support for them to complete their respective programmes of study, then all members of a college's staff have an obligation to work together as a team to achieve this outcome.

The RACI model (Brue 2006), outlined below (Figure 9.1), further examines effective teamwork in teaching.

Subject Tutor

Highlights a potential
issue due to irregularity,
e.g. poor attendance.
Passes on to Personal
Tutor and is kept
INFORMED

Specialists

Could include
support workers,
disability specialists,
parents and Social
Services. They are
CONSULTED

Personal Tutor

Approaches issue
with learner to
determine nature
of problem.
As the learner's
mentor she is
RESPONSIBLE

Principal/Head

Advised of issue by
tutor as they have an
obligation to make
sure support is
accessible. They are
ACCOUNTABLE

Figure 9.1 RACI model

Following this model of effective team work enables an organisation to fully deliver upon their responsibilities to the learner by remembering that these are collective goals, and to attain these we must come to rely on our colleagues within an education setting to each perform their own unique role. The model enables the best qualified person available to contribute to a positive outcome through effective problem solving. In this instance, the message put forth is that teachers should not attempt to overexert themselves and feel compelled to go beyond their job role if they are uncomfortable in doing so, or if they do not believe that they have the relevant training.

Effective teamwork also lends itself to increased professionalism; having established regulations in place to promote a manner of due process within a college also makes it easier for teachers to deliver upon their legislative obligations to safeguard learners etc. A college's organisational rules and procedures help to maintain order and uphold a planned, prepared and structured environment. Issues such as professional objectivism and emotional detachment are also advocated.

Similarly, teachers have both individual responsibilities (with regard to their own teaching methods and planning of teaching and learning activities) and collective responsibilities (legislative, administrative, etc.) that will either have a direct or indirect effect on the college's operational output. Yet no matter what these responsibilities are, whether departmental, organisational or corporate in nature, they are in such abundance given the vague nature of the teaching remit, that they are surely best achieved through working together rather than tackled individually.

The most positive effect of effective team building in teaching is that it shares a seemingly unconquerable workload within an organisation, with tasks distributed appropriately. Some teaching practitioners may criticise investing time and effort into learners in terms of their emotional wellbeing in order to facilitate their education, and while traditionally it may not be regarded as the responsibility of the educator to concern themselves with such issues, recent progressive attitudes suggest that although it may not be our responsibility, we are morally compelled to take it in the best interest of the learner.

If motivational and inspiring lessons are the measure of an outstanding teacher inside of the classroom, then outside of the classroom effective teamwork and communication must be the hallmark of a true professional. Effective teamwork aims to minimise procrastination, and in doing so produce a planned and informed approach when seeking to achieve collective goals; stresses the importance of drafting this approach in full cooperation with legislative and corporate obligations; encourages the best from all involved in the organisation, and motivates professionals towards the best possible outcome for all through focusing efforts on delivering an action plan that has the full commitment of all teachers.

Balancing home-life, study and work

The biggest challenge many of us face is how to balance the demands of family, friends, and career. Working life can be emotionally and physically demanding and can impact on family life, health and well-being. Avoiding burnout by balancing job and family is vital. Your personal life adds dimensions to your professional life and vice versa.

Reflection and activity

Consider how you balance the demands of family, friends and career.

You may have noted the following points:

* Set up a work plan on a daily/weekly/monthly schedule
* Consider what is right for you
* Accept the hard fact that you can't do it all
* After work, try not to take any work home with you
* Use valuable time to relax and rejuvenate by getting proper rest, eating healthily, and having some good times with family and friends
* Take time out for you.

Below, sociology teacher Lucy Dale shares her experience of balancing work and home life.

I have been teaching for seven years now, mainly in the adult sector but I did spend a year teaching 16–19 Sociology AS level. My degree is in Social Science, so I specialise in Psychology and Sociology and have taught across a variety of courses including Access, BTEC and a level 2 course entitled 'Pathfinder'. I have now broadened my teaching to include BTEC Health and Social Care. I live with my three children, partner and our very special tomcat 'Thomas'.

When I first started teaching, I struggled greatly with the work/life balance. Teaching was new to me and being somewhat of a perfectionist I found it hard to know when enough was enough. My children (now 15, 12 and 2) were also a huge part of my life and finding the extra time now required for preparation and marking was hard in terms of having less time for them.

I found myself constantly comparing my life to other teachers. How many hours did they work? How many children did they have? How long did they stay up at night preparing for lessons? Did they have *any* life outside the two?

Finally, I found my own equilibrium and realised that no amount of comparison would help me. I simply had to figure out my own happy work/life balance. Yes, there may be some Supermums (or Dads) out there who can teach a 40-hour week and bring up four children single-handedly with a spot-free home and a perfectly co-ordinated work wardrobe, but it's not me. Also, others may struggle with the demands of teaching without the added pressure of small people living in their home, demanding unlimited amounts of attention.

For me that work/life balance is currently working on a 0.5–0.7 contract freeing me up to give enough time and energy to both my students and my children. For you, it may be that you can juggle more hours, or you need to work less, but only you can decide that for yourself. The key is to feel that you are delivering the best you can to both students and family; the balance will vary and comparing yourself to others only confuses the matter.

Some key skills that are essential to develop to get this right include:

- Organisation – without this you are fighting a losing battle (children will always throw unpredictability into the equation so the more organised you are with the controllable events, the better you will cope).
- Prioritisation – knowing what needs doing and what can be left is essential; things that seemed important before can now take a back seat. (Does that lounge carpet really need hoovering *every* day?)
- Time management – we often don't start a task because we perceive the time allocated not to be enough; however any progress is better than none. No, you can't mark those 20 essays in the 30 minutes you have free before the children arrive home, but you could get five of them done . . .
- Multi-tasking – I don't mean in the important areas, like quality time with your loved ones, or delivering a lesson. But while you are cooking tea, stick a wash on. Or use that time travelling in on the train to go over your lesson plans, do some marking. It's amazing how much you can get done whilst doing something else.

    And finally . . .

- Relax! – work/life balance only works if you have a life! At the beginning it was all work and no play and pretty quickly I found myself dreading the 'half-term meltdown'. Leaving myself no time to recuperate and renew I found I had little to give anyone else. Yes, that lesson tomorrow is important but how can you deliver it effectively if you stay up until three in the morning marking last week's essays?

Continuing Professional Development (CPD)

Keeping up-to-date with research, policy and new initiatives can be a big ask for many busy teachers, made even more difficult in the face of the frequent and changing landscape of Lifelong Learning (see Chapter 2). Maintaining your continued professional development (CPD) can be an important tool for keeping up-to-date, taking ownership of your CPD and being personally and professionally empowered. Strategies to take ownership of your CPD include:

- getting involved in practitioner research (see Tummons and Duckworth 2012)
- becoming a subject specialist coach
- subscribing to a subject-specific journal
- attending conferences
- keeping up-to-date with your reflections
- speaking to your mentor
- planning your CPD for the year so it can be costed into the institutions budget
- registering on a CPD module at a college or university
- joining a community of practice or starting a community within your institution/local community.

Practitioner research

There are various definitions in the literature for practitioner research; it may even be called different names, ranging from participatory action research to action research, to practitioner-led inquiry, or community action research, but there are some shared characteristics that distinguish it from other research methods. In the context of education it can be conducted by the teacher or group of teachers that assumes a dual role, both as teacher and as researcher. It is typically carried out for the purpose of advancing practice. It offers a reflective and systematic approach to research that places a study setting (for example, a FE college or school) and participants (for example, learners) at the heart of the study. It incorporates the collective knowledge of the educational community, and increases the likelihood that results will be applied, for example, in learning and teaching.

Below I describe my experience of partaking in research, whilst working in a college in the North-West of England.

I worked as a literacy teacher within a busy college and had a heavy workload. Within this context, the space I had for critical reflection and innovative practice was very limited. My drive came from the knowledge that education can be truly life enhancing and transforming if appropriate mechanisms are put in place to push open spaces that create a meaningful enquiry into the learners' lives (Duckworth 2013).

Practitioner Action Research (PAR) has been a key part in driving my practice forward. For example, rather than presuming to know what the learners want to learn and what type of resources are best, I began to listen more closely to the learners' voices, letting their needs, aspirations and dreams shape the lessons. As a teacher and researcher I was able to utilise the research findings, which included the link between violence, literacy and learning to inform my classroom practice and create a holistic curriculum driven by the learners' collaboration (see McNamara 2007; Duckworth 2008).

My progression through the research was also supported by the community of practice (Lave and Wenger 1991; Wenger 1998; Wenger et al. 2002) in which I was involved. This included: Research and Practice in Adult Literacy (RaPAL)[1] and North West dialogue.[2] I was also North West Convener for the Learning and Skills Research Network (LSRN)[3] and continue to be a member. The concept of learning communities draws on a wide body of theory related to learning and sociology. They relate to a constructivist approach to learning that recognises the key importance of exchanges with others, and the role of social interactions in the construction of values and identity. For example, the sharing of values in the RaPAL community includes sharing more critical approaches to teaching basic skills and thereby encourages people to reclaim their own learning processes by building their own learning from their own experiences. Later I was inspired by colleagues at Edge Hill University. Each of the communities has supported and contributed to my knowledge and practice, offering a critical space to reflect and develop my own professional practice and identity as a teacher, activist and researcher. Lave and Wenger define a community of practice as follows:

> In using the term community, we do not imply some primordial culture-sharing entity. We assume that members have different interests, make diverse contributions to activity, and hold varied viewpoints. In our view, participation at multiple levels is entailed in membership in a community of practice. Nor does the term community imply necessarily co-presence, a well-defined, identifiable group, or socially visible boundaries. It does imply participation in an activity system about which participants share understandings concerning what they are doing and what this means in their lives and for their communities.
>
> (Lave and Wenger 1991: 97–8)

The Learning and Skills Improvement Service (LSIS) is also host to a number of communities of practice. For example, LSIS has collaborative workrooms to explore your specialist area. The Collaborative Action Research Network (CARN), with regional networks, also supports practitioner research:

- for action researchers working both individually and in collaboration with others
- for anyone wishing to set up action research activities as part of ongoing developments, new inquiries, research projects, community engagements, and so forth
- for anyone who is interested in developing collaborative, critical and creative dialogue between practice and inquiry, research and practice, theory and experience.

CARN supports networking:

- through sharing accounts of action research, on the CARN website, in the Educational Action Research international journal, and through other CARN publications
- through attentive personal encouragement and critical feedback
- through regional events, study days and at the CARN annual conference (http://www.esri.mmu.ac.uk/carnnew/).

Communities of practice can be real or virtual and include online forums, internal and external networks. They can be based on your work team or a cross-organisational group with a shared focus. As my own experience highlights, the support offered by these networks can be both refreshing and vital in sustaining the energy and commitment to both teaching, keeping up-to-date with research, policy and initiative changes in the sector and your professional development.

Reflection and activity

Join a community of practice or set one up in your organisation/ community.

Final thoughts

To engage and enthuse your learners to become empowered, you need to be empowered yourself and take charge of your own professional growth. A dynamic and questioning stance to your own learning will support you to model the attitudes you wish to promote among your learners. Don't be afraid to take risks; remember teaching is a journey of discovery – so enjoy it!

Further reading

Ball, S.J. (2003) The teacher's soul and the terrors of performativity. *Journal of Education Policy*, 18(2): 215–28.

Gibbs, P. (2007) Practical wisdom and the workplace researcher. *London Review of Education*, 5(3): 223–36.

Scales, P., Pickering, J., Senior, L., Headley, K., Garner, P. and Boulton, H. (2011) *Continuing Professional Development in the Lifelong Learning Sector*, Maidenhead: Open University Press.

Tummons, J. and Duckworth, V. (2012) *Doing your Research Project in the Lifelong Learning Sector*, Maidenhead: Open University Press.

Websites

Further education jobs: http://www.fejobs.com, on http://www.fecareers.co.uk and on http://www.teachfe.com

Research and practice in Adult Literacy: http://www.literacy.lancs.ac.uk/rapal/

TLRP (2008), *Education, knowledge and the knowledge economy:* http://www.tlrp.org/pub/documents/globalisationcomm.pdf

Notes

1 Established in 1985, RaPAL is the only British national organisation that focuses on the role of literacy in adult life. An independent network of learners, teachers, managers and researchers in adult basic education it campaigns for the rights of all adults to have access to the full range of literacies in their lives and offers a critique of current policy and practice arguing for broader ideas of literacy starting from theories of language and literacy acquisition that take account of social context. It encourages a broad range of collaborative and reflective research involving all participants in literacy work as partners whilst supporting democratic practices whereby students are central to a learning democracy and their participation in the decision-making processes of practice and research is essential.

2 The aim of North West Dialogue was to create a forum where individuals and organisations in the North West could share and develop research and practice adult SfL. It encouraged the development of research by establishing networks and circulating information across communities of practice.

3 Established in 1997 LSRN was supported by the Learning and Skills Development Agency. It entered a new phase in April 2006 in which it works collaboratively with multiple partner organisations. It is a network based in the regions of England and Northern Ireland. It brings together people involved in producing and making use of research in the learning and skills sector and higher education.

Appendices

Scheme of work

Great Teacher Further Education College

Qualification: AS Level

Course Code: PSYB2 Social Psychology, Cognitive Psychology and Individual differences.

Unit: Social Influence 3.2.1

Number & Length of Sessions:
10 * 1 hour sessions (E Block)
10 * 1.5 hour sessions (B block)

Number of Weeks: 5

Mode of Study: Full Time

Centre: Millennium

Year/Group:
Streamed depending on the GCSE results for Maths, Science, English Lang, History and Geography. These subjects have skills which are required for Psychology.

Aims:

- To provide an introduction to theoretical and methodological approaches in social psychology.
- To demonstrate ways in which social psychology may be applied to contemporary social and cultural issues.
- To enable students to develop critical and evaluative skills in relation to theory and empirical studies in social psychology.
- To develop an appreciation of how science works in social psychology.

Functional Skills:

- *English and communication*
  1. Reading and interpreting skills
  2. Speaking, listening and communicating
  3. Written skills
  4. Language (meta)
- *Mathematics and application of number*
  1. Fractions and percentages
- *ICT*
  1. Direction to Moodle VLE

Every Child Matters:

1. Be healthy
2. Stay safe
3. Enjoy & achieve
4. Make a positive contribution
5. Achieve economic well-being

Safeguarding and signposting:

- Policies followed
- Classroom rules
- Counselling service
- Signposting to external services
- Additional learning support for learning difficulties

Equality and Diversity:

- Religious festival outlined on SOW
- Resources
- Topics discussed

Week	Session	Date w/c	Topic/Content — WHAT	Teaching and Learning strategies (including differentiation) — HOW	Resources — WHAT WITH	Assessment — HOW WILL LEARNING BE CHECKED	ECM	Functional Skills Eng/Com	Functional Skills Maths/AON	Functional Skills ICT	Equality and Diversity
1	1	16.01.12	Conformity: Compliance, internalisation, normative social influence and informational social influence.	Card sort activity using workbooks to become familiar with the terms and definitions (small groups) Scenario worksheet activity to identify the type of conformity and explain why (small groups) Write examples of conformity in workbook Answer past exam questions (written) Sandwich diagram (P.E.E.) to help structure past exam questions (written) Throw ball to facilitate Q and A (verbal)	• Workbooks pp. 4–7 • Prezi • Card sort • Scenario worksheet • Sandwich diagram • Blow up ball	• Q and A (verbal) • Card sort • Identifying examples of conformity • Answer past exam question (written) • Scenario worksheet • Sandwich diagram • Directed study	2, 3, 4, 5	1, 2, 3, 4		–	World religion day (19.01.12) Prezi contains diverse images Card sort and Scenario worksheet contain diverse names All learning styles catered for

(Continued overleaf)

Scheme of work (Continued)

Week/Session	Date w/c	Topic/Content	Teaching and Learning strategies (including differentiation)	Resources	Assessment	ECM	Functional Skills Eng/Com	Functional Skills Maths/AON	Functional Skills ICT	Equality and Diversity
		WHAT	HOW	WHAT WITH	HOW WILL LEARNING BE CHECKED					
2		Pebbles in a jar and Asch study	Post-it notes with written definitions and examples are posted around the room. Use to fill in empty table Peer assess past exam questions set for directed study Pebbles in a jar. Complete experiment by splitting class into two conditions (A and B) Introduce Asch and show video	• Workbooks pp. 7–15 • Prezi • Post-it notes with terms on • Empty table worksheet for terms and definitions • http://www.youtube.com/watch?v=QcmvbXgmdsU&feature=endscreen&NR=1 • Sherif handout	• Q and A (verbal) • Completed terms and definitions worksheet • Peer assessment • Answer past exam questions (written) • Directed study	1, 3	1, 2, 3, 4	1	1	Post-it notes contain diverse names Can discuss Autism – counting Realia – more concrete All learning styles catered for

2	3	23.01.12	Factors which affect conformity	Peer assess past exam questions set for directed study	• Workbooks pp. 11–15	• Q and A (verbal)	1, 3, 4, 5	1, 2, 3, 4	—	—	New Year (Chinese: 23.01.12)
					• Prezi	• Peer assessment					St Paul's Day and St Dwynwen's Day (Christian: 25.01.12)
				Factors worksheet. Work in small groups to complete: name the factor, explain what it is, link to research studies and link to conformity explanation (written). Write responses on the whiteboard so all learners can compile	• Factors worksheet	• Answer past exam questions (written)					
					• Whiteboard and pen	• Completed factors worksheet					National Holocaust Memorial Day (27.01.12)
					• Deluxe worksheet	• Identifying examples					
				Complete examples in workbook (written)		• Directed study					Lower ability learners only need to know 2 of the 4 factors in detail
				Answer past exam questions (written)		• Completed deluxe worksheet					
				Use deluxe worksheet to summarise the session							

(Continued overleaf)

Scheme of work (Continued)

Week Session	Date w/c	Topic/Content	Teaching and Learning strategies (including differentiation)	Resources	Assessment	ECM	Eng/Com	Maths/AON	ICT	Equality and Diversity
		WHAT	**HOW**	**WHAT WITH**	**HOW WILL LEARNING BE CHECKED**			Functional Skills		
4		Conformity explanations and factors essays	Complete crossword Peer assess past exam questions set for directed study Small group task – answer two of the questions on the explanations worksheet. Feedback to the class	• Workbooks pp. 15–17 • Prezi • Crossword hand-out • Explanations essay worksheet • Factors essay worksheet • Post-it notes	• Q and A (verbal) • Completion of crossword • Peer assessment • Small group activity for explanations • Small group activity for factors • Directed study • Target plenary	2, 3, 5	1, 2, 3, 4	–	–	Higher ability learners will be able to complete the whole crossword. Lower ability learners will benefit more from the consolidation afterwards Group work allows scaffolding of learners Plenary allows for individual targets

| 3 | 5 | 30.01.12 | Conformity explanations and factors essays | Small group task – answer two of the questions on the factors worksheet. Feedback to the class

Set essays for directed study

Complete a post-it with answers to 3 questions on learning – targets

Complete conformity summary worksheet in small groups. Use Prezi and whiteboard to consolidate

Discuss essay plans

Peer assess past exam essay questions set for directed study

Complete past exam essay question in exam conditions 20 mins

Triptico recap activity | • Workbooks pp.18–19
• Prezi
• Conformity summary worksheet
• Whiteboard and pen
• Triptico | • Q and A (verbal)
• Completion of conformity summary sheet
• Peer assessment
• Marked essay questions
• Answers to Triptico | 2, 3, 5 | 1, 2, 3, 4 | – | – | Birthday of Guru Har Rai (Sikh: 31.01.12) |

(Continued overleaf)

Scheme of work (*Continued*)

Week Session	Date w/c	Topic/Content	Teaching and Learning strategies (including differentiation)	Resources	Assessment	ECM	Functional Skills Eng/Com	Functional Skills Maths/AON	Functional Skills ICT	Equality and Diversity
		WHAT	**HOW**	**WHAT WITH**	**HOW WILL LEARNING BE CHECKED**					
6		Obedience and defiance	Starter activity to ask learners to obey trivial commands such as stand up, pull ear, etc. Introduce to Milgram and show video Whilst watching the video learners to complete worksheet with questions on. Stop the video half way to ensure have the answers and repeat at the end Complete storyboard for Milgram study	• Workbooks pp. 18–19 • Prezi • http://www. youtube.com/ watch?v=ZB8 AMUHq2HY • Milgram video worksheet • Storyboard worksheet	• Q and A (verbal) • Completion of Milgram video worksheet • Completion of storyboard • Directed study	1, 3, 5	1, 2, 4	–	–	Learners can choose to draw or write the details of the study dependent on learning style/ preference All learning styles catered for

			Activities	Resources	Assessment			Notes
4	7	06.02.12	Explanations for obedience	Go through help sheets for the conformity essays and return marked essays Peer assess directed study Answer past exam questions (written) Card sort activity Direct to workbook to discuss Milgram Authoritarian Personality as an explanation. Direct to interactive of scale activity Label explanations activity	• Workbooks pp. 20–31 • Prezi • Explanations feedback handout • Factors feedback handout • Marked essays • Card sort • Explanations worksheet	• Q and A (verbal) • Completion of card sort • Completion of explanations worksheet • Directed study	1,3,4,5	1,2,3,4	Teng Chieh (Chinese: 06.02.12) Parinirvana/ Nirvana Day (Buddhist: 08.02.12) Tu B'Shevat (Jewish: 08.02.12) Lower ability learners only need to know 2 of the 4 factors in detail Group work allows scaffolding

(Continued overleaf)

Scheme of work (*Continued*)

Week Session	Date w/c	Topic/Content	Teaching and Learning strategies (including differentiation)	Resources	Assessment	ECM	Eng/Com	Maths/AON	ICT	Equality and Diversity
		WHAT	**HOW**	**WHAT WITH**	**HOW WILL LEARNING BE CHECKED**					
8		Factors which affect obedience	Peer assess past exam questions set for directed study Work in pairs to complete the Hofling and Bickman worksheet (written) Work in small groups to complete one factor and consolidate on the whiteboard (written) Answer past exam questions (written) Plenary Q and A of session	• Workbooks pp. 25–31 • Prezi • Hofling and Bickman worksheet • Factors worksheet • Whiteboard and pen • Test your knowledge worksheet	• Q and A (verbal) • Peer assessment. • Completion of Hofling and Bickman worksheet • Completion of factors worksheet • Directed study	1, 3, 4, 5	1, 2, 3, 4	1	1	Differentiated questioning

Week	Lesson	Date	Topic	Activities	Resources	Assessment				Notes
5	9	20.02.12	Obedience explanations essay	Show Petcha Kutcha slide show to illustrate obedience cross-culturally Peer assess test your knowledge worksheet set for directed study Discuss plan for the essay Complete past exam essay question in exam conditions 20 mins	• Petcha Kutcha • Prezi • Explanations questions worksheet	• Q and A (verbal) • Peer assessment • Completion of the essay question	1, 3, 5	1, 2, 3	—	Maha Shivaratri (Hindu: 20.02.12) Shrove Tuesday (Christian: 21.02.12) Ash Wednesday and Lent (Christian: 22.02.12)
	10		Obedience factors essay	Triptico recap activity Peer assess past exam questions set for directed study Discuss plan for the essay Work in pairs to write half of the essay. Then join another pair to complete the essay. Peer assess and add feedback	• Triptico • Prezi • Factors questions worksheet	• Answers to Triptico • Q and A (verbal) • Peer assessment • Completion of the essay question	1, 3, 5	1, 2, 3	—	Discussion of obedience around the world: US and Nazi Germany

Post Compulsory Education and Training Session Plan

Course	AS level. PSYB2 Social Psychology, Unit 3.2.1: Social Influence.
Week No/ Session Title	17. Social Influence: Dominant Response Theory.
Date & Time	19.03.12 Monday 13.30–15.00
Location	Psychology department of great teaching
Tutor/s	Samantha Jane Catterall
Duration	1 hour and 30 mins.
Aims	• To provide an introduction to theoretical and methodological approaches in social psychology. • To demonstrate ways in which social psychology may be applied to contemporary social and cultural issues. • To enable students to develop critical and evaluative skills in relation to theory and empirical studies in social psychology. • To develop an appreciation of how science works in social psychology.
Objectives	By the end of the session all learners will be able to: LO1: Name and explain careers in psychology. LO2: Identify 10 correct statements relating to social facilitation. LO3: Describe a study in which social facilitation was investigated. LO4: Name 3 theories of social facilitation. LO5: Name a study which supports the dominant response theory. LO6: Explain what social facilitation/inhibition is. By the end of the session most learners will be able to: LO4: Explain the dominant response theory of social facilitation. LO5: Describe a study which supports the dominant response theory (Aim, Method, Results and Conclusion). LO6: Discuss why social facilitation/inhibition occurs due to dominant response theory.

Differentiated Learning	Learners who are early can watch videos about careers.
	Various tasks to allow higher ability learners to expand and use higher order cognitive skills. Easier tasks to allow lower ability learners to achieve. Debate allows learners to choose what type of answer to give.
	Learning objectives are differentiated to demonstrate all learners can achieve in the session.
Notes	Nominated questioning is differentiated so that higher ability learners are stretched by allowing them to expand on their answers and lower ability learners can be asked more closed and directive questioning. SC is diabetic and therefore may need to leave the classroom during the session for a short time.

(Continued overleaf)

Post Compulsory Education and Training Session Plan (*Continued*)

Approximate Timings	Learning Objectives	Learner Activity	Teacher Activity	Resources	Assessing Learning
Start: 13.30 (5 mins)		Answer verbally. Listening.	Take a register. Go through session outline. Play videos.	Register. PowerPoint. YouTube.	Verbal response.
13.35 (10 mins)	LO1	Complete starter. Answer questions verbally.	Ask questions verbally.	Career starter diagram. Career PowerPoint.	
13.45 (10 mins)	LO2	Select 10 of the correct statements.	Split into 2 teams. Flip a coin to decide who goes first.	Triptico. Handout. PowerPoint.	
13.55 (10 mins)	LO3	Change directed study with another learner. Answer questions verbally.	Direct learners to change directed study with another learner. Ask questions verbally.	PowerPoint Workbook p. 3	
14.05 (5 mins)	LO4	Answer questions verbally.	Recap the 3 theories of social facilitation. Ask questions verbally.	PowerPoint. Workbook p. 4	

Time	LO	Activity	Teaching	Resources	Assessment
14.10 (15 mins)	LO5	Work in groups of 4 to write the aim, method, results and conclusion for Michaels et al. Study and answer exam question in the middle.	Show diagram. Direct to complete task.	PowerPoint. Flipchart paper and pens.	Written completion of the flipchart paper.
14.25 (15 mins)		Feedback to the class. Stand up and hold up work.	Nominate learners to feedback. Write response on board.	Whiteboard and pen. Prezi/PowerPoint.	Verbal response.
14.40 (10 mins)	LO6	If holding the ball must make a point.	Debate: Social facilitation versus social inhibition.	PowerPoint. Ball.	Verbal response.
14.50 (5 mins)	ALL	Complete the card and post it through suggestion box.	Direct to complete and return.	Feedback form.	Written completion of the form.

Evaluation :

Targets for improvement

Identify your **SMART** targets for improving your teaching and classroom management

1.
2.
3.

(Continued overleaf)

Post Compulsory Education and Training Session Plan *(Continued)*

Functional Skills		E.L.M.
	Functional English: - Written skills will be developed when completing the group work task. - Speaking, listening and communication skills will be developed when working with other learners to complete the Michaels et al. Study task, when feeding back to the class, answering questions and during the debate. - Reading and interpreting skills will be developed when using the workbooks to help complete the Michaels et al. Study task. **Functional Mathematics** - Equivalencies such as fractions and percentages will be discussed when referring to the results of studies. **Functional ICT** - Learners can take pictures of the board at any time.	**Be Safe:** Health and Safety is followed such as learners sitting properly on chairs. **Be Healthy:** Learners' interaction with each other when completing the small activity and the class discussions will promote social and emotional health. **Enjoy and Achieve:** Learners will be included within the session and given the opportunity to achieve by asking questions and taking part in the small group task and class discussions. **Achieving economic wellbeing:** Learners are aware of the benefits of teamwork and communication and how these relate to employment. The small group work in this session helps develop these skills. **Making a positive contribution:** Learners are encouraged to take part in all aspects of the session to build their confidence and allow them to feel confident in taking part in their community outside of the session.

Practical Presentation Skill Level 2 Progression

Name... Group.....................................

Give three reasons why presentations may be necessary.

Describe the most common delivery styles and structures for presentations (PowerPoint etc.).
Explain the importance of:

a) Preparation;
b) Planning;
c) Presentation;
d) Performance.

Describe the main elements that make up each of the above.
   Describe a variety of visual aids for use within given presentations, giving reasons for selection.
   Checklist for your presentation:

1. Identify and select different sources of information relevant to the topic of presentation.
2. Introduce the topic clearly.
3. Speak audibly, using tone and register appropriate to the audience and level of formality.
4. Present material logically, linking ideas together.
5. Present an effective conclusion.
6. Explain key concepts.
7. Use appropriate evidence to support the ideas, argument and opinions presented.
8. Assess own performance.
9. Obtain feedback from audience.
10. Identify areas for own improvement.

Bibliography

Andresen, L.W. (1994) *Lecturing to Large Groups*. SEDA: Paper 81.

Argyris, C. and Schön, D. (1974) *Theory in Practice: Increasing Professional Effectiveness*. San Francisco: Jossey-Bass.

Armitage, A., Bryant, R., Dunnill, R., Flanagan, K., Hayes, D., Hudson, A. and Kent, J. (2003) *Teaching and Training in Post Compulsory Education*. Maidenhead: Open University Press.

Bailey, K., Curtis, A. and Nunan, D. (2000) *Pursuing Professional Development: The Self as Source*. Boston, MA: Heinle & Heinle.

Barton, D. and Hamilton, M. (1998) *Local Literacies: Reading and Writing in one Community*. London: Routledge.

Barton, D., Ivanic, R., Appleby, Y., Hodge, R. and Tusting, K (2006) *Relating Adults' Lives and Learning: Participation and Engagement in Different Settings*. London: NRDC.

Barton, D., Ivanic, R., Appleby, Y., Hodge, R. and Tusting, K. (2007) *Literacy, Lives and Learning*. London: Routledge.

Bathmaker, A.M. and Avis, J. (2005) 'Becoming a lecturer in further education in England: the construction of professional identity and the role of communities of practice' in *Journal of Education for Teaching*, 31(1): 47–62.

Becher, T. (ed.) (1994) *Governments and Professional Education*. Buckingham: Open University Press.

Becher, T. (1994) 'The significance of disciplinary differences' in *Studies in Higher Education*, 19: 151–157.

Becker, H. (1963) *Outsiders: Studies in Sociology of Deviance*. New York: Free Press.

Becker, H.S., Geer, B., Hughes, E.C. and Strauss, A.L. (1961) *Boys in White*. Chicago, IL: University of Chicago Press.

Benner, P. (1984) *From Novice to Expert: Excellence and Power in Clinical Nursing Practice*. California: Addison-Wesley.

Biggs, J.B. (1999) *What the Student Does: Teaching for Quality Learning at University*. Buckingham: Open University Press.

Bines, H. (1992) 'Issues in course design' in H. Bines and D. Watson (eds) *Developing Professional Education*. Buckingham: Society for Research into Higher Education and Buckingham University Press.

BIS (Department for Business, Innovation and Skills) (2011) New Challenges, New Chances: Further Education and Skills System Reform Plan: BIS.

Black, P. and William, D. (1998) 'Assessment and classroom learning, assessment' in *Education: Principles, Policy & Practice*, 5(1): 7–74 [online at] http://dx.doi.org/10.1080/0969595980050102

Blatchford, P. (1996) 'Pupils' views on school work and school from 7–16 years' in *Research Papers in Education*, 11(3): 263.

Bligh, D. (2000) *What's the Use of Lectures?* London: Jossey-Bass, Wiley.

Bloom, B.S. (1956) *Taxonomy of Educational Objectives: Book 1 Cognitive Domain*. New York: Longman.

Bowles, S. and Gintis, H. (1976) *Schooling in Capitalist America*. London: Routledge.

Braverman, H. (1974) *Labour and Monopoly Capital: The Degradation of Work in the 20th Century*. New York: Monthly Review Press.

British Dyslexia Association (2010) http://www.bdadyslexia.org.uk/about-us.html (accessed 17 November 2012).

Brockbank, A. and McGill, I. (1999) *Facilitating Reflective Learning in Higher Education*. London: SRHE and Open University Press.

Brookfield, S.D. (1995) *Becoming a Critically Reflective Teacher*. San Francisco, CA: Jossey-Bass.

Brown, G. (1980) *Lecturing and Explaining*. London: Methuen.

Brown, P. (2008) Teaching and Learning Research Briefing, October 2008, no. 53 http://www.tlrp.org/pub/documents/BrownRB53final.pdf.

Brown, S. and Race, P. (2002) *Lecturing: a Practical Guide*. London: Routledge Falmer.

Brue, G. (2006) *Six Sigma for Small Business*. Madison, WI: CWL.

Bruner, J. (1985) 'Vygotsky: a historical and conceptual perspective' in J.V. Wertsch (ed.), *Culture, Communication and Cognition: Vygotskian Perspectives*. Cambridge: Cambridge University Press.

Bruner, J. (1990) *Acts of Meaning*. London: Harvard University Press.

Burrage, M. (1994) 'Routine and Discrete Relationships: Professional Accreditation and the State in Britain' in Becher, T. (ed.) (1994) *Governments and Professional Education*. Buckingham: Open University Press.

Burrage, M. and Torstendahl, R. (eds) (1990) *Professions in Theory and History: Rethinking the Study of the Professions*. London: Sage.

Buzan, T. (2003) *Use Your Head*. London: BBC.

Bynner, J. and Parsons, S. (2005) *New Light on Literacy and Numeracy*. London: National Research and Development Centre for Adult Literacy and Numeracy.

Bynner, J. and Parsons, S. (2006) 'New light on literacy and numeracy' in *Reflect On-line*, Issue 4, available at http://www.nrdc.org.uk/content.asp?CategoryID=922 (accessed 4 December 2012).

Campbell, A., McNamara, O. and Gilroy, P. (2004) *Practitioner Research and Professional Development in Education*. London: Paul Chapman.

Carr, W. (1995) 'What is an educational practice?' in *For Education*. London: Open University Press.

Carr-Saunders, A.M. and Wilson, P.A. (1933) *The Professions*. Oxford: Clarendon Press.

Casey, H., Cara, O., Eldred, J., Grief, S., Hodge, R., Ivanivic, R., Jupp, T., Lopez, D. and McNeil, B. (2007) 'You wouldn't expect a maths teacher to teach plastering . . .' Embedding literacy, language and numeracy in post-16 vocational programmes – the impact on learning and achievement. Summary Report, NRDC.

Clarke, J. and Newman, J. (1997) *The Managerial State*. London: Sage.

Cohen, M. and Sproull, L.S. (1996) *Organisational Learning*. London: Sage.

Colley, H., James, D. and Diment, K. (2007) 'Unbecoming teachers: towards a more dynamic notion of professional participation' in the *Journal of Education Policy*, 22(2): 173–193.

Collier, P.J. and Morgan, D.L. (2007) '"Is that paper really due today?" Differences in first-generation and traditional college students' understandings of faculty expectations' in *Higher Education*, 55(4): 425–446.

Commission for Health Improvement (2003) *The Victoria Climbié Report: Key findings from the self audits of NHS organisations, social services departments, and police forces*. London: The Stationery Office.

Deliberations Website: http://www.lgu.ac.uk/deliberations/home.html

DfE (2010) *The Importance of Teaching: The Schools White Paper 2010*. London: DfE.

DfEE (1998) *The Learning Age: a Renaissance for a New Britain* (Green Paper CM 3790). London: The Stationery Office.

DfEE (1999) *A Fresh Start: The report of a working group chaired by Sir Claus Moser*. London: DfEE.

DfEE (2001) Executive Summary of *Skills for Life: The national strategy to improve adult literacy and numeracy skills*. Nottingham: DfEE.

DfES (2002) *Success for All*. London: DfES.

DfES (2004) *Equipping our Teachers for the Future*. London: DfES.

DfES (2005) *Realising the Potential – A review of the future role of further education colleges (The Foster Report)*. Nottinghamshire: DfES. Available online at: http://www.dfes.gov.uk/furthereducation/fereview/downloads/REALISING06.pdf

DfES (2006) *Further Education: Raising Skills, Improving Life Chances*, Cm 6768, Norwich: The Stationery Office. Available online at: http://

www.dfes.gov.uk/publications/furthereducation/docs/6514-FE%20 White%20Paper.pdf

Department for Business, Innovation and Skills (2010) *URN 10/1274 Skills for Sustainable Growth. Full Report.* Available at: http://www.bis. gov.uk/assets/biscore/further-education-skills/docs/s/10-1274-skills-for-sustainable-growth-strategy.pdf (accessed on 10/09/2012).

Department for Education and Skills (DfES) (2005) Realising the Potential – A review of the future role of further education colleges (The Foster Report), Nottinghamshire: DfES.

DfE (2011) *Training our next generation of outstanding teachers.* London: DfE.

DfE (2012) Wolf Report response. Available at: http://media.education. gov.uk/assets/files/pdf/w/wolf%20review%20of%20vocational%20 education%20%20%20government%20response.pdf (Accessed 04/12/ 2012).

Dewey, J. (1910) *How We Think.* Lexington, MA: D.C. Heath.

Dewey, J. (1938) *Experience and Education.* New York: Macmillan.

Dreyfus, H.L. and Dreyfus, S.E. (1986) *Mind over Machine: The Power of Human Intuition and Expertise in the Era of the Computer.* Oxford: Blackwell.

Dreyfus, S. (1981) 'Formal models vs human situational understanding.' Schloss Laxenburg, Austria, Institute for Applied Systems Analysis.

Duckworth, V. (2008) *Getting Better Worksheets, Adult Literacy Resources.* Warrington: Gatehouse Books.

Duckworth, V. (2010) 'Sustaining learning over time: It looks more like a Yellow Brick Road than a straightforward path for women experiencing violence' in *Research and Practice in Adult Literacy*, 71: 19–20.

Duckworth, V. (2013) *Learning Trajectories, Violence and Empowerment amongst Adult Basic Skills Learners. Education Research Monograph.* London: Routledge.

Duckworth, V. and Cochrane, M. (2012) 'Spoilt for choice, spoilt by choice: Long-term consequences of limitations imposed by social background' in *Education and Training*, 54(7): 579–591

Duckworth, V., Flannagan, K., McCormack, K. and Tummons, J. (2012) *Understanding Behaviour 14+.* Maidenhead: McGraw-Hill Education.

Duckworth, V., Gelling, C., Sheridan, B., and Shiel, C. (2010) *I teach: Journeys into Teaching.* Warrington: Gatehouse Books.

Duckworth, V. and Taylor, K. (2008) 'Words are for Everyone' in *Research and Practice in Adult Literacy*, 64: 30–32.

Duckworth, V. and Tummons, J. (2010) *Contemporary Issues in Lifelong Learning.* Maidenhead: Open University Press.

Ecclestone, K. (1994) 'Reflective practice – model or mantra?' *Conference Paper UCLAN.*

Education and Skills Act – explanatory notes. Available at: www.opsi.gov. uk/acts/acts2008/en/ukpgaen_20080025_en_1.htm

Elliott, J. (2007) *Reflecting Where the Action Is: The Selected Works of John Elliott*. London and New York: Routledge.

Equality Act (2010) Available at: http://www.legislation.gov.uk/ukpga/ 2010/15/contents (accessed 18/12/2012).

Eraut, M. (1994) *Developing Professional Knowledge and Competence*. London: Falmer.

Etzioni, A. (ed.) (1969) *The Semi Professions*. New York: Free Press.

Evetts, J. (2009) 'New professionalism and new public management: changes, continuities and consequences' in *Comparative Sociology* 8(2): 247–266.

Exley, K. and Dennick, R. (2004) *Giving a Lecture: From Presenting to Teaching*. London: Routledge.

Field, J. (2000) *Lifelong Learning and the New Educational Order*. Stoke-on-Trent: Trentham Books.

Field, J. (2010) *Equality in a Time of Change*. Dublin: The Equality Authority.

Finlay, I., Spours, K., Steer, R., Coffield, F., Gregson, M. and Hodgson, A. (2007) '"The heart of what we do": policies on teaching, learning and assessment in the new learning and skills sector' in *Journal of Vocational Education and Training*, 59(2): 137–153.

Fiszer, E.P. (2003) '*How Teachers Learn Best: An Ongoing Professional Development Model*.' Rowman & Littlefield Publishers.

Forster, F., Hounsell, D. and Thompson, S. (eds) (1995) *Tutoring and Demonstrating: a handbook*. Edinburgh: UCOSDA.

Foster, A. (2005) *Realising the Potential: A review of Further Education Colleges*. London: DFES.

Foucault, M. (1977) *Discipline and Punish: The Birth of the Prison*. London: Allen Lane.

Freire, P. (1993) *Pedagogy of the Oppressed*. New York: Continuum.

Further Education Teachers' Qualifications (England) Regulations 2007 (SI 2007 No. 2264. Available at: http://www.legislation.gov.uk/uksi/ 2007/2264/contents/made).

Gee, J.P. (2001) 'Identity as an analytic lens for research in education' in *Review of Research in Education*, 25: 99–125.

Gibbs, G. (1981) 'Twenty terrible reasons for lecturing', SCED Occasional Paper 8.

Gibbs, G. (1988) *Learning by Doing*. Oxford: FEU.

Gibbs, G. (1992) *Lecturing to More Students*. Oxford: PCFC.

Gibbs, G. and Jenkins, A. (1992) *Teaching Large Classes in Higher Education*. London: Kogan Page.

Giroux, H. (1997) *Pedagogy and the Politics of Hope: Theory, Culture, and Schooling*. Boulder, CO: Westview.

Goode, W.J. (1957) 'Community within a community: the professions' in *American Sociological Review,* 22: 194–200.

Goodlad, S. (ed.) (1984) *Rethinking Professional Education – Quis custodiet . . .?* London: NFER-Nelson.

Halsey, A.H. (1992) *Decline of Donnish Dominion: the British Academic Profession in the Twentieth Century.* Oxford: Clarendon Press.

Hammersley-Fletcher, L. and Orsmond, P. (2004) 'Evaluating our peers: is peer observation a meaningful process?' in *Studies in Higher Education,* 29(4): 489–503.

Hammersley-Fletcher, L. and Orsmond, P. (2005) 'Reflecting on reflective practices within peer observation' in *Studies in Higher Education*, 30(2): 213–224.

Hancock, M. (2012) Association of Colleges (AoC) http://www.feguild. info/FE%20Guild%20-%20Briefing%20note%20for%20AOC%20 conference%20-%20final.pdf

Hargreaves, D. (1982) *The Challenge for the Comprehensive School.* London: RKP.

Hargreaves, D. (1996) *'Teaching as a Research Based Profession: Possibilities and Prospects.'* Teacher Training Agency Annual Lecture.

Hattie, J. (2009) *Visible Learning: a synthesis of over 800 meta-analyses relating to achievement.* New York: Routledge.

Henkel, M. (1994) 'Social work: an incorrigibly marginal profession?' in Becher, T. (ed.) *Governments and Professional Education.* Buckingham: Open University Press.

Hirst, P.H. (1974) *Knowledge and the Curriculum.* London: Routledge and Kegan Paul.

Hirst, P.H. (1993) 'Education, Knowledge and Practices', in R. Barrow and P. White (eds) *Beyond Liberal Education.* London: Routledge.

HM Government (2003) *Green Paper: Every Child Matters.* See: (https:// www.education.gov.uk/publications/standard/publicationDetail/Page1/ CM5 86 (accessed August 2012)).

HM Government (2011) Review of Vocational Education: The Wolf Report. London: Department for Education.

Hodkinson, P. (1992) 'Alternative models of competence in vocational education and training' in *Journal of Further and Higher Education,* 16 (2): 30–39.

hooks, bell (1994) *Teaching to Transgress: Education as the Practice of Freedom.* London: Routledge.

Hyland, T. (1995) *Competence, Education and NVQs: Dissenting Perspectives.* London: Cassell.

Illich, I. (1973) *Deschooling Society.* Harmondsworth: Penguin.

Illich, I. (1975) *The Disabling Professions.* London: Penguin.

Ingle, S. and Duckworth, V. (2013) *Enhancing Learning through Technology in Lifelong Learning: Fresh ideas; Innovative Strategies.* Maidenhead: Open University Press.

Jaques, D. (2000) *Learning Groups* (3rd edn). London: Kogan Page.

Johns, C. (1994) 'Nuances of reflection' in *Journal of Clinical Nursing* 3: 71–75.

Jones, L. and Moore, R. (1993) 'Education, competence and the control of expertise', in *British Journal of Sociology of Education*, 14(4): 385–397.

Kennedy, H. (1997) *Learning Works*: the report of the Further Education Funding Council committee on widening participation in Further Education (June 1997, FEFC).

Knight, J. (1997) *Strategic Planning for School Managers*. London: Kogan.

Knowles, M.S. (1980) *The Modern Practice of Adult Education: From Pedagogy to Andragogy*. Chicago: Follett.

Knowles, M.S. (1984) *The Adult Learner: A Neglected Species* (3rd edn). Houston: Gulf.

Knowles, M. (2005) *The Adult Learner* (6th edn). Burlington, MA: Elsevier.

Kolb, D. (1984) *Experiential Learning – Experience as the Source of Learning and Development*. New Jersey: Prentice Hall.

Kolb, D.A., Rubin, I.M. and Macintyre, J.M. (1984) *Organisational Psychology: An Experiential Approach*. New Jersey: Prentice Hall.

Lankshear, C. (1993) 'Functional literacy from a Freirean point of view', in McLaren, P. and Leonard, P. (eds), *Paulo Freire: A Critical Encounter*, pp. 90–118. New York: Routledge.

Lankshear, C. and McLaren, P. (eds) (1992) *Critical Literacy: Politics, Praxis, and the Postmodern*. Albany, NY: State University of New York Press.

Larsen, M.S. (1977) *The Rise of Professionalism – A Sociological Analysis*. Berkeley: University of California Press.

Lave, J. and Wenger, E. (1991) *Situated Learning: Legitimate Peripheral Participating*. Cambridge: Cambridge University Press.

Leathwood, C. (2006) 'Gendered constructions of lifelong learning and the learner in the UK policy context', in Leathwood, C. and Francis, B. (eds) *Gender and Lifelong Learning: Critical Feminist Engagements*, pp. 40–53. London: Routledge.

Leggatt, T. (1970) 'Teaching as a profession' in J.A. Jackson (ed.) *Professions and Professionalization*. London: Cambridge University Press.

Leitch, S. (2006) *Prosperity for all in the global economy world class skills*. Final report of the Leitch Review of Skills. London: HMSO/HM Treasury.

Lifelong Learning UK (LLUK) (2011) *New Overarching Professional Standards for Teachers, Tutors and Trainers in the Lifelong Learning Sector*. London: LLUK.

Lingfield Report (2012) Available at: https://www.gov.uk/government/uploads/system/uploads/attachment_data/file/34641/12-1198-professionalism-in-further-education-final.pdf (Accessed on 04/01/2013).

Lumby, J. and Foskett, N. (2007) *14–19 Education Policy, Leadership and Learning*. London: Sage.

Macedo, D. (1994) *Literacies of Power: What Americans are not Allowed to Know*. Boulder, CO: Westview.

Manpower Services Commission (1981) *A New Training Initiative: An Agenda for Action*. MSC.

Maslow, A. (1993) *The Farther Reaches of Human Nature*. London: Penguin Arkana.

McGill, I. and Beaty, E. (1995 second edition, reprinted 1998) *Action Learning: A Guide for Professional, Management and Educational Development*. London: Kogan Page.

McKeachie, W.J. (2002) *McKeachie's Teaching Tips*. New York: Houghton Mifflin.

McNamara, M. (2007) *Getting Better*. Warrington: Gatehouse Books.

Mellar, H., Kambouri, M., Logan, K., Betts, S., Nance, B., and Moriarty, V. (2007) *Effective Teaching and Learning: Using ICT*. London: NRDC.

Millerson, W. (1964) *The Qualifying Associations: A Study in Professional Development*. London: Routledge and Kegan Paul.

Moon, J. (1999) *Learning Journals: A Handbook for Academics, Students and Professional Development*. London: Routledge Falmer.

National Committee of Inquiry into Higher Education (1997) *Higher Education in the Learning Society*. London: NCIHE.

NCVQ (1991) *Criteria for National Vocational Qualifications*. London: National Council for Vocational Qualifications.

Norris, N. (1991) 'The trouble with competence' in *Cambridge Journal of Education*, 21(3): 331–341.

Ofsted (Office for Standards in Education) (2012a) *The Framework for School Inspection*. Available at: http://www.ofsted.gov.uk/resources/frameworkfor-school-inspection-january-2012.

Ofsted (2012b) Consultation Document: Common Inspection Framework. Available at: http://www.ofsted.gov.uk/resources/common-inspection framework-2012.

Otter, S. (1994) *Higher Level NVQs/SVQs: Their Possible Implications for Higher Education*. Sheffield: DfEE.

Parmenter, D. (2007) *Key Performance Indicators: Developing, Implementing and Using Winning KPIs*. Hoboken, NJ: Wiley & Sons.

Peery, A.B. (2004) *Deep Change: Professional Development from the Inside Out*. Lanham, MD: Rowman & Littlefield Publishers.

Perkin, H. (1989) *The Rise of Professional Society England since 1880*. London: Routledge.

Perry, E. and Francis, B. (2010) *The Social Class Gap for Educational Achievement: A review of the Literature.* RSA Projects, available at: www.thersa.org/-data/assets/pdf_file/0019/367003/RSA-Social-Justice-paper.pdf

Petty, G. (2009) *Teaching Today: A Practical Guide* (4th edn). Cheltenham: Nelson Thornes.

Phenix, P. (1964) *Realms of Meaning.* New York: McGraw-Hill.

Pring, R. (1984) *Personal and Social Education in the Curriculum.* Sevenoaks: Hodder and Stoughton.

Ramsden, P. (1992) *Learning to Teach in Higher Education.* London: Routledge.

Reay, D., David, M.E. and Ball, S. (2005) *Degrees of Choice: Social Class, Race and Gender in Higher Education.* Stoke-on-Trent: Trentham Books.

Reece, I. and Walker, S. (2007) *Teaching, Training and Learning – A Practical Guide.* London: Business Education Publishers Limited.

Rogers, A. (2002) *Teaching Adults* (3rd edn). Maidenhead: Open University Press, McGraw-Hill Education.

Rogers, C. (1969) *Freedom to Learn.* Columbus, Ohio: Bell and Howell.

Rogers, C. (1996) *Way of Being.* New York: Houghton Mifflin Company.

Sambell, K., McDowell, L. and Montgomery, C. (2012) *Assessment for Learning in Higher Education.* Abingdon: Routledge.

Saunders, M. (1995) 'The integrative principle: higher education and work based learning in the UK' in *European Journal of Education* 30(2): 203–216.

Saunders, M. (2000) 'Beginning an evaluation with RUFDATA: theorizing a practical approach to evaluation planning' in *Evaluation* 6(1): 7–21.

Saunders, M. (2006) 'From "organisms" to "boundaries": the uneven development of theory narratives in education, learning and work connections' in *Journal of Education and Work* 19(1): 1–27.

Saunders, M., Fulton, O. and McNugh, G. (1990) Report: Work-based Learning and Its Accreditation: Can Higher Education Deliver? CSET, Lancaster University.

Scales, P. (2007) *Teaching in the Lifelong Learning Sector.* Maidenhead: Open University Press.

Schön, D.A. (1983) *The Reflective Practitioner.* London: Temple Smith.

Schön, D.A. (1987) *Educating the Reflective Practitioner.* London: Jossey-Bass.

Senge, P.M. (1990) *The Fifth Discipline.* New York: Doubleday/Currency.

Shor, I. (1992) *Empowering Education: Critical Teaching for Social Change.* Chicago: University of Chicago Press.

Shor, I. (1993) 'Education is politics: Paulo Freire's critical pedagogy', in McLaren, P. and Leonard, P. (eds) (1993), *Paulo Freire: A critical encounter*, pp. 25–35. London: Routledge.

Siegrist, H. (1994) 'The professions, state and government in theory and history' in Becher, T. (ed.) (1994) *Governments and Professional Education*. Buckingham: Open University Press.

Skinner, B.F. (1953) *Science and Human Behaviour*. New York: Macmillan.

Stanton, G. and Fletcher, M. (2006) *14–19 Institutional Arrangements in England: A research perspective on collaboration, competition and patterns of post-16 provision*. Nuffield Review Working Paper 38.

Stenhouse, L.A. (1971) *Culture and Education*. London: Nelson.

Stenhouse, L. (1975) *An Introduction to Curriculum Research and Development*. London: Heinemann.

Sterling, B. (2005) *Shaping Things*, Mediawork Pamphlet Series, Cambridge, Massachusetts: MIT Press.

Stobart, G. (2005) 'Fairness in multicultural assessment systems' in *Assessment in Education: Principles, Policy and Practice*, 12(3): 275–287.

Taylor, W. (1994) 'Teacher education: Backstage to centre stage' in Becher, T. (ed.) *Governments and Professional Education*. Buckingham: Open University Press.

T.E.A.C.H. report (2007) *A Report from the Historical Association on the Challenges and Opportunities for Teaching Emotive and Controversial History*. London: Historical Association.

Teaching and Learning Research project (TLRP, 2007) *Principles into Practice: A teacher's guide to Research Evidence on Teaching and Learning*. London: Institute of Education

Teaching and Learning Research project (TLRP, 2008), *Education, knowledge and the knowledge economy*, Research briefing No 53. London: Institute of Education.

Tett, L., Hall, S., Maclachlan, K., Thorpe, G., Edwards, V. and Garside, L. (2006) *Evaluation of the Scottish Adult Literacy and Numeracy (ALN) Strategy*. Edinburgh: Scottish Executive Social Research.

Thomas, L., Bland, D. and Duckworth, V. (2012) 'Teachers as advocates for widening participation' in *Widening Participation and Lifelong Learning*, 14(2): 40–58.

Tomlinson, J. (1996) *Inclusive Learning*. Further Education Funding Council: HMSO.

Troman, G. (2007) 'Research on teachers' work and teacher professionalism: a short history' in I. Hextall, A. Cribb, S. Gewirtz, P. Mahony and G. Troman (eds) *Changing Teacher Roles, Identities and Professionalism: An Annotated Bibliography*. London, Kings College/Roehampton University.

Tummons, J. and Duckworth, V. (2012) *Doing your Research Project in the Lifelong Learning Sector*. Maidenhead: Open University Press.

UKCES (2010) *Ambition 2020: World Class Skills and Jobs for the UK*. Available at: http://www.ukces.org.uk/upload/pdf/UKCES_FullReport_USB_A2020.pdf

Wellington, B. and Austin, P. (1996) 'Orientations to reflective practice' in *Educational Research,* Vol. 38 (3): 307–316.

Wenger, E. (1998) *Communities of Practice, Learning, Meaning and Identity.* Cambridge: Cambridge University Press.

Wenger, E., McDermott, R., and Snyder, W.M. (2002) *Cultivating Communities of Practice.* Boston, MA: Harvard Business School Press.

Wilensky, H. (1964) 'The professionalization of everyone' in *American Journal of Sociology,* 70: 137–158.

Winter, R. (1993) *Outline of a General Theory of Professional Competences.* Chelmsford: Anglia Polytechnic.

Wolf, A. (2011) The Wolf Report. Available at: https://www.education.gov.uk/publications/eOrderingDownload/The%20Wolf%20Report.pdf (accessed 04/12/2012).

Wragg, E.C. (1999) *An Introduction to Classroom Observation* (2nd edn). London: Routledge.

Zembylas, M. (2003) 'Emotions and Teacher identity: A poststructural perspective. Teachers and teaching' in *Theory and Practice,* 9: 213–238.

Websites

DfE (2010) The importance of teaching – the Schools White Paper 2010, https://www.education.gov.uk/publications/standard/publicationdetail/page1/CM%207980.

Ofsted (2011) Common Inspection Framework 2012: consultation document (110070), www.ofsted.gov.uk/resources/110070

Ofsted (2012) *Subsidiary guidance,* www.ofsted/resources/110166

Index